D1616024

THIS IS THE AFGHAN HOUND

By Joan McDonald Brearley

Distributed in the U.S.A. by T.F.H. Publications, Inc., 211 West Sylvania Avenue, P.O. Box 27, Neptune City, N.J. 07753; in England by T.F.H. (Gt. Britain) Ltd., 13 Nutley Lane, Reigate, Surrey; in Canada to the book store and library trade by Clarke, Irwin & Company, Clarwin House, 791 St. Clair Avenue West, Toronto 10, Ontario; in Canada to the pet trade by Rolf C. Hagen Ltd., 3225 Sartelon Street, Montreal 382, Quebec; in Southeast Asia by Y.W. Ong, 9 Lorong 36 Geylang, Singapore 14; in Australia and the south Pacific by Pet Imports Pty. Ltd., P.O. Box 149, Brookvale 2100, N.S.W., Australia. Published by T.F.H. Publications, Inc. Ltd., The British Crown Colony of Hong Kong.

Frontispiece:

Ch. Sahadi Shikari, top-winning Afghan Hound in America for 1963, and fifth ranking of all hound breeds, according to the Phillips system. This glorious black dog, owned by Dr. and Mrs. Earl Winter, has six specialty shows and five all-breed best in show wins to his credit to date. Bred by Joan Brearley, "Sheik" is a son of Ch. Shirkhan of Grandeur, out of Ch. Crown Crest Khalifah. Photo by Joan Ludwig.

ISBN 0-87666-231-9

About the Author

Joan McDonald Brearley has been attracted to animals since she was five years old, at which impressionable age she ran away to a zoo. Then followed a succession of pet dogs, cats, birds, fish, rabbits, snakes, turtles, baby alligators, squirrels, lizards, hamsters, etc., for her own personal menagerie. Through the years she has owned over twenty different breeds of pure-bred dogs and countless mixtures, since the door was never closed to a needy or homeless animal.

A graduate of the American Academy of Dramatic Arts, Joan started her career as a dancer, actress, and writer for movie magazines, and still writes professionally for magazines and television, including some of the top personalities in show business. Her dog writings include columnist for *Popular Dogs* magazine for five years, correspondent for *Inu-Nu-Saki*, the Japanese dog world magazine, and the *American Kennel Gazette*.

Breeding and showing Afghan Hounds since 1955, Joan has been active as a member, and on the Board of Directors, of the Afghan Hound Club of America, the Kennel Club of Northern New Jersey, the Stewards Club of America, and is a licensed American Kennel Club dog show judge.

Joan's Sahadi Kennels and Cattery are located in Englewood, New Jersey, and at present count include fourteen Afghan Hounds, two Yorkshire Terriers, and six show cats, several of which are professional models and are seen in top magazines and on television. Besides her activities in caring for animals, Joan spends much time at the art galleries, the theatre, the opera, the typewriter, and—the zoo.

ACKNOWLEDGMENTS

This glimpse into the history of the Afghan Hound would not have come about had it not been for the influence of several important people. First, Kay Finch at whose knee I learned to love and care for our favorite breed; to Ernest H. Hart for his magnificent cover portrait of Ch. Sahadi Sadruddin, and for his artistic contributions throughout the book; to Robert R. Shomer, D.V.M., for expert counsel over the years; to William H. A. Carr, for more reasons than I can count here; and to my parents, who instilled in me my great love for animals which has been the joy of my life.

CONTENTS

Ch. Crown Crest Khalifah, owned by the author, pictured at nine and a half years.

This book is fondly dedicated to
CH. CROWN CREST KHALIFAH
the foundation of my Sahadi Kennels, one of the
top-producing Afghan Hound bitches in the world,
and my dearest friend.

Introduction

To know an Afghan Hound is to love one . . . and you are to be considered fortunate to be able to enjoy the pleasure of their company. If you are about to purchase your first Afghan Hound you are to be congratulated! You have selected a breed rich in history, high in intelligence, and possessed of the ultimate in beauty and grace of motion. The Afghan Hound is all this, and more.

You will find your Afghan Hound is as happy draped langorously on sofa or chair as he is on the track of a hare in the brush or of a lion or gazelle in the mountains. Afghan Hounds are affectionate, yet at times outrageously aloof. They are completely clownish one moment, somber as the Sphinx the next.

Not only is the Afghan Hound of today in more beautiful coat than ever before in his romantic history, but he also does not shed, does not bark any more than he deems absolutely necessary, and does not have the doggy odor associated with dogs in general and hounds in particular.

Even though today's Afghan Hound is not called upon to hunt for his own or his master's food, to zealously defend the entrances to ancient walled cities, or to patrol the outskirts of nomadic desert caravans, you will discover he still retains the innate desire to guard his home and family proudly, as he has done in centuries past. He is an excellent hunter and a worthy companion, and he has established a place for himself as a top show and obedience contender in the dog world.

It is the hopeful purpose of this book to introduce the breed to potential fanciers, presenting the fundamentals of care, habits, and

The author with Ch. Crown Crest Jesi Jhaimz, her first Afghan, her first champion, the first stud dog at her Sahadi Kennels.

history. It is also the purpose of this book to give the long-time devotees of the breed an up-to-the-minute record of this illustrious dog.

I invite all dog lovers to share in this royal heritage and to join other Afghan Hound lovers, Afghan Hound breeders, and Afghan Hound exhibitors the world over in our sincere and dedicated efforts to preserve the integrity of this exotic breed in the centuries to come.

Joan McDonald Brearley
SAHADI KENNELS, REG.
Englewood, New Jersey

Chapter I
Ancient History of the Breed

THE ORIGIN OF THE AFGHAN HOUND

Some three thousand years before Christ, when the warring northern and southern kingdoms of Egypt were uniting under the reign of King Menes to form the First Dynasty of Egypt, the acknowledgment of the existence of a slender hound of the Afghan type was first being recorded on papyrus and portrayed in hieroglyphics on the walls of the pyramids of the gods in Egypt's Valley of the Kings.

Ch. Seria of Scheherezade and her kennel mate, Ch. Alibaba of Scheherezade, owned by Lt. Col. Wallace Pede of Virginia, pose in a magnificient fireside study.

11

Archeological histories estimate the actual existence of the breed as long ago as seven thousand years, with its origin seeming to center around the Mountain of Moses on the Sinai Peninsula. There are also historical theories on additional evidences of simultaneous appearances of the same type of dog all over the Asian continent as well.

In Afghanistan, whence the dog derives its name, it is regarded, though unofficially, as the "national dog," and native Afghans claim and believe this monkey-faced, or baboon, dog, as it was often called, was the chosen dog to accompany Noah on his ark in the year of the great flood. They also uphold the belief that it is the dog portrayed

Ch. Majara Mudarris (deceased) was sired by the great Ch. Ali Khyber, and was owned by Dr. and Mrs. Frederick Clarke.

Three generations of Stormhill champions. Ch. Stormhill Silver Dream, Ch. Stormhill San-Dhal, his daughter, and San-Dhal's daughter, Ch. Pandora of Stormhill, all bred, owned, and handled by Virginia Withington.

in the rock carvings on the walls of the caves in the northern province of Balkh. This is the reason it has also been referred to as the Balkh Hound.

The correct interpretation of these ancient and obscure carvings, and the conjecture regarding the Afghan Hound's being the only dog mentioned in the New Testament of the Bible, will always be open to argument, or personal opinion. And it is sure to be the basis of heated discussion when Afghan fanciers get together.

But we do know this: the Afghan type dog goes back so far that historian Jackson Sanford, in a scientific paper, states that the Afghan Hound represents a form of animal structure found on earth over one hundred thousand years ago. Based on bone structure comparisons, it is a contemporary of the very earliest Asian dog-like animals which

A glamorous headstudy of the showring and obedience ring winner, Ch. Crown Crest Khittiku, C. D. Retired shortly after her second birthday for breeding purposes, Khittiku has several champion offspring to her credit. Photo by Frasie.

Ch. Pandora of Stormhill, owned, bred and handled by Gini Withington, has 4 best in show wins, and 37 hound group firsts to date, as well as the Chicago and Northern California Specialty Show wins to her credit. Pan, continues her winning ways across the country as top winning bitch in the breed. Photo by Joan Ludwig.

are believed to have inhabited even the North American continent two millions years ago.

In the earliest written records of the breed, however, there is almost a habit of "mixing and matching" the Afghan Hound with the Greyhound and the Saluki, with points of variance being mainly the outward appearances of each, namely, coat and feathering. There is much reference to what might easily be a composite of all three throughout these histories. It is only when man began to analyze the work each species was expected to perform in the different countries and climates that we see the Afghan Hound begin to emerge and develop as the superior hunter because of its coat, long-range eyesight, and "pivotal hipjoints."

Arnold Fletcher, one-time Deputy Director of Habibia College in Kabul, Afghanistan, claims that a Greyhound's legs would have snapped on the quick turns necessary when doubling back on prey, but the almost pivotal hipjoints of the Afghan Hound enable it to turn almost within the length of itself. Also, the smooth-coated Greyhound fell subject to respiratory diseases in extremely cold temperatures of the upper snow regions, whereas the Afghan Hound prospered under the protection of its heavy coat.

While this profusion of coat guarded it against the cold, it also shielded this fleet-footed mountain hunter from the merciless sun while it coursed the desert. With its huge, thickly-padded paws and powerful hindquarters, the Afghan Hound was also the perfect "desert dog," with equal ability to skin across the hot desert sands or to scale rocky tors in the mountainous territory.

Ch. Tarylane's Mr. Wonderful, bred by Ray Schmidt, named for the play of the same name, and owned by Ellen Steinschneider. Photo by Stephen Klein.

This charming, informal study shows young Christopher Tongren and three furry friends at play at the ben ghaZi Kennels.

In order to pinpoint the origin and purpose of this dog down through the centuries we must remember that the Afghan Hound of the past did not present the same picture it does today. The beautifully-coated well-fed Afghan Hounds that give rise to the choruses of *Oh's* and *Ah's* in today's show ring certainly are not representative of the breed in acient times. The appearance has changed, and so has the purpose to which the dog is put. We must recall the differences in the borderlines of the countries during past centuries. Constantly moving native tribes and traders kept national borders irregular and indistinct. But each "country," even as it was then, found its own use and purpose for this hound in its ultimate scheme of life.

In Egypt, for instance, where only a select few animals such as the Brahman bull and the cat were revered, the Afghan-type dog won

17

sovereignty for itself by becoming a companion to kings, and came to play a significant part in the national religion. Legend has it that a dog guided Isis, goddess of motherhood and fertility, when she searched for her brother and husband, Osiris, a wise king of Egypt who was brutally murdered and tossed into the Nile by his brother. The role played in his most triumphant return and his elevation to the status of a great god also immortalized the dog in the land of the Pharaohs.

Even beyond this royal role as companion to kings, these Egyptian dogs were used as guards, walking sentry duty each night with an eye for raiding tribes creeping in from the desert to steal. Sleeping by day and walking guard in pairs at night around the oases and cities, the Afghan Hounds were also taught to steal from neighboring encampments for the good of their masters. This is a trait that has remained with the Afghan Hound through the centuries. Present-day Afghan Hound owners readily admit that their dogs are expert at thievery, and that every pure-bred Afghan Hound still harbors a bit of larceny in its soul!

In the Middle Ages, dog teams were used to pull carts of cloth, tea, furs, incense, and other commodities between Persia, India, Arabia, Russia, and China. They seem to have penetrated as far north as Scandinavia and as far east as China. Woodcuts after Olaus Manus depicting Scandinavian hunters on skis armed with crossbows in the 16th century show dogs bearing a strong resemblance to the Afghan Hound running alongside them.

Examples of Asian art bear out the appearance of this type of dog in Chinese sculpture and carved jade. The Cairo Museum is reported to have on display a piece of pottery bearing Afghan-like creatures in chase which was unearthed along with other treasures from King Tutankhamen's tomb.

THE AFGHAN HOUND IN AFGHANISTAN

In Afghanistan the dog excelled as a hunter. Hunting is, and always has been, the most popular pastime in Afghanistan. Wealthy Afghans, aboard their excellent horses, equipped with guns and hounds, hunt expressly for sport. At times they also employ falcons which ride on their gauntlets until released to swoop down and distract the prey as it is chased and surrounded by the dogs.

Afghan Hounds are primarily sight (as well as scent) hunters. They have exceptional vision and can spot prey far off before using their

Ch. Patterson's Hermes, owned by Connie Patterson. He is a full litter brother of Ch. Patterson's Artemis. The sire of these two glorious Afghan Hounds was Ch. Majara Marfu.

fantastic running speed, estimated at twenty-five miles or more per hour at full speed, to track down what they have spotted. Sometimes hunting in pairs, male and female, the female usually chooses to circle the prey, bounding and barking wildly to distract it while the male awaits the opportunity to leap at the prey's throat, where he hangs on until the neck is snapped and broken. Their great speed and power enables them to hunt gazelles, snow leopards, wolves, hyenas, and jackrabbits and animals of similar size. Their powerful twisting jaws make a kill almost certain.

The poorer people of Afghanistan, however, hunt for the most primeval of reasons . . . for food and skins. With the tribesmen, however, the Afghan Hound is taught to hunt without devouring or killing the catch, but merely to keep it at bay, allowing the master to deliver the death blow so that the game may be eaten without sacrilege. According to the Mohammedan religion, only slaughtered game may be consumed.

Ordinary dogs in Afghanistan are regarded as unclean and are often clubbed and stoned in the streets. But the Afghan Hound is admired and respected by all without exception. To the rich he is a skilled and swift hunter, and to the poor he is an invaluable guard and provider of food and clothing.

Whatever the Afghan Hound's use or purpose has been down through the centuries, it has withstood the changing sands of time and has remained a dog of great intelligence and beauty. While written records might be inadequate, incomplete, or even questionable, it is generally agreed that the exotic Afghan Hound is of the pre-Christian era.

Chapter II
Modern History

EUROPEAN HISTORY

Strangely enough, we have World War I to thank for popularizing the Afghan Hound with European dog lovers. If it hadn't been for the war, when Great Britain sent armed forces to the far-flung corners of the globe, an Afghan Hound might not have crossed the path of

Frederick T. Daws, the prominent English artist, painted this oil of four Afghan Hound greats. From left to right are Ch. West Mil Omar of Prides Hill, Ch. Badshah of Ainsdart, Int. Ch. Sirdar of Ghazni, and in the foreground, Ch. Azri Havid of Ghazni. Marion Foster Florsheim brought this painting to the United States from England. It now is proudly displayed in a place of honor in Kay Finch's living room.

Ch. Sirdar of Ghazni, pictured in this reproduction of the famous oil painting done in 1927 by artist F. T. Daws. Sirdar has been referred to as the "father" of the breed, winning fame in England as a potent sire as well as a show dog.

Captain John Barff, who imported the famous Zardin to England from the Seistan province, in the Far East.

Zardin proved to be a sensation in Britain, so much so that he was requested for a personal appearance before Queen Alexandra at Buckingham Palace. Brought out of quarantine after his importation, he proceeded to win the foreign dog class at the British Crystal Palace in 1907 and was undefeated in fifty-two consecutive shows. Pictures in old English dog chronicles refer to Zardin's offspring as Persian Greyhounds, or Afghan Greyhounds, as they were often called in Asian countries. But Zardin obviously carried the full coat, topknot, and ringed tail that some of the first importations at the turn of the century had not carried.

Captain Barff sold Zardin to a London animal dealer who bred him to bitches also imported by Captain Barff, but unexplained circumstances wiped out all Afghan Hound stock the animal dealer had, and nothing further was ever learned of Zardin's progeny. It has been rumored that Zardin's remains are at rest in the British Museum, but a friend of mine, a researcher on the staff of the zoology department, reports she can find no trace. Just a photograph of Zardin had been there, and even this was not recovered after the devastating bombings of London during World War II. She has located mounted skins, formerly on exhibition but now in storage, of two Afghan Hounds named Shadzadia and Mooroo, presented to the museum in 1901 by a Mrs. Whitbread. I am indebted to Mrs. S. M. Harding, known professionally as Dr. Manton, for her investigations. Nevertheless, it was with this famous show-winning dog in mind that the original standard for the breed was established.

Zardin, the first Afghan brought to England. He was brought to the British Isles in the latter part of the nineteenth century. The sensation he caused then can still be felt in the breed today.

Ch. Kazan's Makari, owned by Mr. and Mrs. Edwin L. Smith.

The first Afghan Hound Club of America match show, held at the Five Mile Kennels of Marion Florsheim, on September 26, 1941. Judge John H. Hill awarded best in match honors to Mrs. Sherman Hoyt's Rudika of Blakeen.

One of the old greats, and winner of the parent club specialty in 1942 and 1943, Ch. Rajah of Arken, owned by Lillian and Charles Wernsman.

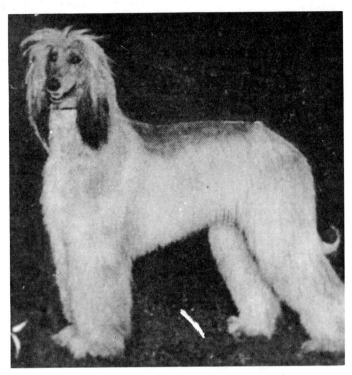

Ch. Egypt's Echo of Crown Crest, owned and bred by Kay Finch. This exquisite Afghan was the dam of seven champions. Photo by Joan Ludwig.

The names of military men keep popping up in the annals of the early importations. Time and again we see not only the name of Captain Barff but also the names of Captain F. Martin, Captain Cary Barnard, Colonel Marriott, and Major Mackenzie as being responsible for bringing these unusual dogs back to England. With their distinctive appearance and winning ways, Afghan Hounds brought with them a reputation of being great hunters and the ability to course at fantastic speeds, as well as an assortment of names ranging from Tazi or Thasi, to Kurrum or Baluchi Hounds, to Barukhzy Hounds, derived from the name of the family of hunters who bred them for hunting lions in Afghanistan.

Quite naturally a dog breed with a reported running speed of twenty-five miles an hour or more was bound to be mentioned in racing circles. In 1937 Mrs. Molly Sharpe brought out a string of her

Int. Ch. Badshah of Ainsdart, one of the early Afghan Greats. He was very important to the beginning of the breed's popularity in the United States.

Afghan Hounds to race. Perhaps the most famous was her International Champion Garrymhor Faiz-Bu-Hassid, often photographed in a completely horizontal line, so far straight out ahead and to the rear were his legs while racing. As early as 1933 Afghan Hounds were being primed for coursing hare, and when they proved to be extremely fast, a Coursing Club was formed.

Until this remarkable dog arrived in the British Isles the Greyhound had the edge on racing. But an interesting incident occurred which proved that the Greyhound enthusiasts had to bow to the speed of the Afghan Hound. Clifford Hubbard, in his British book *The Afghan Hound*, relates that a red bitch named Baz, imported for a Mr. N. Dunn by an Indian Army officer who purchased her from a desert caravan, was bred to a Greyhound named Explosion with the explicit purpose of giving additional stamina to the Greyhound.

What is perhaps even more incredible, Baz was eventually registered in the Greyhound stud book in 1911, by special resolution of

Ch. Zarif of Hu-Ed, C.D., Winners Dog at the Afghan Hound Club of America Specialty Show in 1953, and one of the first obedience titled Afghan Hounds. Owned by Mr. and Mrs. Edwin L. Smith.

Another of the all-time Afghan Hound "greats," Ch. Garrymhor Zabardast of Arken, owned by the Arken Kennels.

the National Coursing Club! It is also interesting to know that the get of this strange breeding all carried the Afghan Hound ringed tail!

The very earliest importations to England that laid the groundwork for Zardin's subsequent success appeared even before the turn of the century. An Afghan Hound named Gazelle was, with another dog, the winner of second prize in the foreign dog class at the Crufts

Dog Show in 1895. Other wins at other dog shows followed, and in 1897 there were two Afghan Hound entries. One was a dog named Dilkoosh, who oddly enough appeared in the stud book as an Afghan Bamkhzy Hound!

There are also reports that Major Mackenzie had a foreign dog class winner at Bristol in his Mukmul. The Major took a second place win later on at the Barn Elms show in 1887 with his bitch Moroo. Major Mackenzie imported many Afghan Hounds around the turn of the century and was considered an authority in the breed. His Khulm caused quite a stir, and Captain Cary Barnard's Afghan, Bob, was popular at the time. But none was to cause the comment evoked by the great Zardin.

The importing of new stock to Britain ceased during the actual hostilities of World War I, but it wasn't long after the treaty was signed that the far-sighted Miss Jean Manson and Major and Mrs. Bell-Murray reached to the Far East for new blood to import as foundation stock for their kennels. Several studs and brood bitches were selected and sent to England. These were later to become the prominent names on the pedigrees of European Afghan Hounds in the early 1920's.

Ch. Zair Zina of Kandullah

In 1925 the first Afghan Hound Club was formed in England by Miss Evelyn Denyer, a prominent Afghan Hound kennel owner who also served as the club's first secretary. It was this original breed club that prepared and presented the official Afghan Hound standard to the Kennel Club of England, and won championship status for the breed. After this acceptance it was no longer necessary for exhibitors to show their dogs in the foreign dog class at dog shows.

Ch. Zattu of Kandullah

Although this was accomplished in 1925, the first Crufts Challenge Certificates were not awarded until 1926; they were awarded at that time by Judge A. Croxton Smith. One of the first of these Certificates was presented to Miss Jean Manson's Ranee, a cream-colored bitch bred in 1919 by the Bell-Murray Kennels. It was 1927, however, before the first Afghan Hound champion was recorded. Bred by the Bell-Murray Kennels and owned by Jean Manson, Buckmal, a black-masked, wheat-colored dog, was the first Afghan Hound to attain this title in England. In 1929 the first champion bitch was recorded. (Also bred by the Bell-Murray Kennels and owned by Miss Manson was Shadi, a six-year-old bitch that won certificates in Scotland and elsewhere during 1927 as well as her third certificate at Crufts in 1929.)

With the great love and admiration Zardin and some of the other early importations won in England, the breed began to flourish. More and more kennel names began to appear in the Afghan Hound world. One of these still well-remembered names is Ghazni. The Ghazni Kennels, founded by Mary Amps, was the home of the illustrious Ch. Sirdar of Ghazni, one of the best-known sires in

Ch. Turkuman Nissim's Laurel, owned by Sunny Shay and Sol Malkin. This dog was one of the top winners of the breed during the early fifties. Among his many top awards was first in the hound group at the 1950 Westminster Kennel Club.

early Afghan Hound history in Europe. Mrs. Amps purchased and imported this black-masked, true red stud, bred in King Amanullah's royal kennels in Afghanistan, from the British Legation in Kabul, and started him on his show career in 1925.

Sirdar of Ghazni was acclaimed the best specimen of the breed since Zardin, and it was Sirdar upon which the present English Afghan Hound standard is based. Sire of six champions, three champion sons and three champion daughters, his famous name appears on the finest pedigrees for the breed in England and the United States.

A black and tan son of Sirdar, Ch. Asri-Havid of Ghazni, went to Mrs. Phyllis Robson, who was first to win Best In Show honors with an Afghan Hound in England. This honor came in 1934. It was this same dog that was first to win obedience certificates in the Afghan breed as well. Phyllis Robson's first love was Afghan Hounds, and she not only did much to popularize the breed in England but also was a campaigner of purebred dogs and of licensed dog shows; in addition, she edited the internationally famous publication *English Dog World*. Mrs. Robson died in 1959, still working for the good of dogs and praising the beauty of the Afghan Hound.

Sirdar's famous sons in turn produced famous sons, among them Ch. Badshah of Ainsdart, first Best In Show Afghan Hound in the United States. He was sire of International Champion Rudiki of Pride's Hill, whose name appears on the pedigrees of many of America's top-winning show dogs. With these great dogs gaining in popularity, Afghan Hound kennels began to increase their breeding programs. By 1963 over 4,500 Afghan Hounds had been registered in the stud book in the Kennel Club of England.

Ch. Faith, C.D., a beautiful black-masked red bitch, was not only outstanding in the obedience ring, but her show ring career made her the top-winning bitch on the West Coast in 1955. Faith is co-owned by J. E. Robinette and Virginia S. Mika.

The kennels largely responsible for this increase were the Baber-bagh Kennels of Mrs. Prude; Molly Sharpe's Chaman Kennels; Mrs. M. Wood's Westmill; Garrymhor of Mrs. O. M. Couper; Ainsdart, belonging to Mrs. Morris-Jones; Kuranda Kennels of Mrs. Rothwell-Fielding; the Geufron name used by Mrs. Eileen Drinkwater; Mrs. Sydney Rhodes' Tucklo Kennels; Eileen Snelling with the Khorrassan name; Mrs. F. C. Riley's Bletchingley Kennels; Mrs. Edgar Abson's Netheroyd Kennels; and the el Kabul Kennels of Dr. Betsy Porter. Dr. Porter is a frequent visitor to the United States and was invited to judge the Potomac Afghan Hound Club Specialty Show in this country in 1960.

The above mentioned Netheroyd line produced the first black champion bitch, Netheroyd Turkuman Camelthorn, dam of the famous Ch. Turkuman Nissim's Laurel, the black Afghan Hound which won the Afghan Hound Specialty Show in the United States and the Westminster Kennel Club Hound Group in 1950 after he was exported to America. He was shown during his remarkable show ring career by Sunny Shay of the Grandeur Kennels and was co-owned by Sunny Shay and Sol Malkin.

Other European kennels that figured prominently in the history of the breed are the Oranje Manege Kennels (Netherlands) of Miss Eva Pauptit, from whom Mrs. Kay Finch of the Crown Crest Kennels in California imported her great International Champion Ophaal of Crown Crest, the sire of many American champions. Before being imported to this country Ophaal sired some of the outstanding racing dogs still in England. One of these is Arabdur, the record-holding winner of over fifty firsts, including the racing derby and the world show race.

In Norway the Tonnessen Kennels of Oslo are famous for their Afghan Hounds, and they are shown extensively at shows in that country. In Belgium, Mariette Decker's kennel produced Amanullah Khan of Acklam, a beautifully marked black and tan dog distinguished by impressive wins at both French and Belgian shows. In Switzerland the name Stockmann was synonymous with that of the Afghan Hound. In Canada Mary Matchett's beautiful El Myia Afghan Hounds are famous and frequently enter competition in the United States.

While Afghan Hounds have long been known to North Africa, especially Egypt, the man credited with having introduced the breed to South Africa and Rhodesia in recent years is Benjamen R. Spencer

Ch. Sahadi Sequin, owned and shown by Mel McCarthy and Nancy McCarthy Gardner, finished her Championship with four major wins, and has one leg on her C.D. title. Sequin was sired by Shirkhan of Grandeur, out of Ch. Crown Crest Khalifah, and was bred by Joan Brearley.

of the Transvaal. In 1957, on a trip to the United States and Canada to perform several dog show judging assignments, Mr. Spencer revealed that in Africa the Afghan Hound is still first and foremost used for hunting and coursing. Mr. Spencer is onetime chairman of the South African Gun Dog League and has finished four Best In Show Afghan Hounds of his own breeding in South Africa.

HISTORY OF THE BREED IN THE UNITED STATES

The Afghan Hound's beginning in the United States was, fortunately, a very excellent one. Its heritage in this country sprung

Ch. Hope, a glamorous, black-masked, silver bitch, is another of the top-producing bitches in the breed. Hope is the dam of the famous Ch. Crown Crest Mr. Universe, the show-winning record-holder in the history of the Afghan Hound, and has over a dozen champion sons and daughters to her credit. Photo by Joan Ludwig.

from worthy importations of Jean Manson and the Bell-Murray kennel stock, which had been virtually the foundation stock for Britain as well. It is estimated that from 15% to 25% of the United States breeding is founded on the Bell-Murray strain and 20% to 30% on Mary Amp's famous Ch. Sirdar of Ghazni.

In fact, we must acknowledge Miss Manson's breeding behind the very first litter of three Afghan Hound puppies to be registered with the American Kennel Club (in 1926, by the Dunwalke Kennels). The first U.S. registration of a litter bred in this country was made by the Valley Farm Kennels in September of 1928. Parents of the dam of this litter also spring from Miss Manson's breeding.

Importation of two Afghan Hound greats was accomplished in the early 1930's by Zeppo Marx, of the famous Marx Brothers comedy team. He brought them to this country to appear in a movie. Their names were Westmil Omar and Asra of Ghazni. Following their

Crown Crest Raffles, a striking, black-masked, silver dog owned by Charles Farley.

A headstudy of Ch. Crown Crest Babaloo, the foundation bitch of the Davi-Baba Kennels. Photo by William Brown.

movie debut these two exceptional hounds were purchased by George S. Thomas, who later sold them to Q. A. Shaw McKean.

Asra of Ghazni was to become a most prolific producer. Her first litter, of five, was born on April 1, 1932, at Mr. McKean's Pride's Hill farm, with G. S. Thomas listed as the breeder. Before her death at the age of fourteen years, Asra had whelped some seventy-odd Afghan Hounds to help establish the breed in this country.

On the advice of Mr. Thomas, Shaw McKean also purchased the smoke-colored brindle Badshah of Ainsdart, born in 1930. Badshah distinguished himself by becoming the first Afghan Hound to win a Best In Show award in the United States. So enthusiastic did Mr. McKean and a neighbor, Mr. Bayard Warren, become about this fleet-footed breed that they entertained thoughts about racing

A handsome father and son pair of Canadian champions owned by Mary Matchett. On the left, Ch. Kurram El Myia; on the right, Ch. Hindukist El Myia.

Ch. Gitana Del Desierto is from the show and racing kennels of Pearson Crosby. "Gypsy" hunts jack rabbits on the New Mexico desert, leaping from the roof of Mr. Crosby's truck as they cross the open sands. A perfect example of an Afghan Hound that is as good in the show ring as she is on a trail. Photo by Joan Ludwig.

Afghans. First they tried out their hounds on mechanical hares at the Wonderland dog track. That is, they tried them out until the Greyhound owners learned of it and prevailed upon the track management to put a stop to it. Mr. Warren had purchased some of the early Westmil Omar out of Asra of Ghazni puppies from Mr. McKean; he used them to race along with Mr. McKean's hounds.

One of the puppies from this same breeding was Barberryhill Illusion, dam of Barberryhill Dolly, Venita Varden Oakie's famous brood and show bitch. In November of 1932 a repeat breeding of Asra of Ghazni to Westmil Omar was to produce two strong stud dogs for the breed, Mr. McKean's Zahera of Pride's Hill and Kundah of Pride's Hill, the latter being the maternal grandsire of Ch. Rudiki

Ch. Crown Crest Jesi Jhaimz, a beautiful black-masked son and likeness of the fabulous Ch. Taejon of Crown Crest. A sire of champions,
"Jaimie" is owned by Sahadi Kennels.

Pictured in front of the Stormhill Kennels is Ch. Stormhill Silver Dream with three of his champion daughters. Owner Gini Withington holds the reins on this attractive group. Photo by Joan Ludwig.

Ch. Nigro's Zarak, co-owned by Alice Nigro (his breeder) and Frances Karasak. This flashy, black-masked, red son of the renowned Ch. Crown Crest Rubi, has numerous group placings to his credit. Handled by, and pictured here with Robert Forsyth. Photo by Evelyn Shafer.

of Pride's Hill. Rudiki, Badshah, and Zahera are prominent names in pedigrees in this country and are as well known today for their greatness as they were in their heyday.

International Champion Rudiki of Pride's Hill, purchased and owned by Marion Foster Florsheim, was fifteen times a Best In Show winner, twenty-seven times Best-American Bred In Show, forty-times Best Hound, with seventy-three additional group placings, and seventy-seven Best of Breed wins—a truly glorious and most remarkable show record. Reported to be an almost carbon copy of his illustrious grandsire, Ch. Sirdar of Ghazni, Rudiki sired over two hundred puppies in his lifetime. This accounts for his name's appearing on so many of the better pedigrees in the United States. In recent years Mrs. Florsheim has been concentrating on judging, having closed her famous Five Mile Kennels shortly after the death of her beloved Rudiki on Christmas Eve, 1947.

In the 1930's Afghan Hounds began to take hold in popularity in this country, and their devoted supporters began to work diligently at gaining recognition for the breed. Anyone who is sincerely interested in the breed today and does even the most minimal amount of research will find that certain names keep cropping up—names we have all come to acknowledge as the foundation breeders and exponents of the Afghan Hound in their early days in America.

Undeniably, the aforementioned Shaw McKean was the first enthusiast. Mrs. Sherman Hoyt of the Blakeen Kennels, Mrs. Marion Foster Florsheim, Mrs. Jack Oakie of the Oakvarden line, Charles and Lillian Wernsman, Mr. and Mrs. Robert Boger, Leah

Ch. Kurki ben ghaZi, another top-winning Afghan Hound from Mrs. Ruth Tongren's well-known ben ghaZi Kennels. Photo by Evelyn Shafer.

One of the most famous Afghan Hounds of all time, International Champion Rudiki of Prides Hill, with owner Marion Foster Florsheim, at her Five Mile Kennel. Photo by Vandamm.

McConaha, and numerous others were the pioneers of the breed. It is said of Mr. Wernsman that it was a familiar sight to see him arrive at a dog show with practically every Afghan Hound in his kennel aboard with the express purpose of giving the breed a large entry to help the Afghan Hound become recognized with the American Kennel Club.

Obviously this technique, and all the time Charles Wernsman and his wife Lillian took to talk about and glorify the Afghan Hound to prospective comers to this breed, paid off. New names, many of them still prominent today, began to appear: Mrs. Lauer Froelich's Elcoza Kennels; Mrs. William Porter's Kingsway line; Dr. William Iven's Holiday House establishment; the Balmor Kennels of Mr. and Mrs. Lemuel Ayers; Miss White's New Mexico kennel with the Kandahar line; Kay Finch's Crown Crest Afghan Hounds; Marjorie Lathrop's Majara; Sunny Shay's Grandeur Kennels; Ruth Tongren's

Ch. ben ghaZi's Kaman, winner of the 1958 Tara Afghan Hound Club Specialty Show under judge Alys Carlsen. By the end of 1959 Kaman had won twelve group firsts and twenty-three group placings. Kaman was bred by Ruth Tongren at her ben ghaZi Kennels. Photo by Evelyn Shafer.

Ch. Swedika Joh-Cyn, shown winning Best of Breed over champions at Santa Cruz, California under judge Mrs. Helen W. Walsh. Swedika was bred and owned by Mrs. Cynthia Guzevich and is a daughter of the famous Int. Ch. Tanjores Domino, and the equally famous Int. Ch. Tajmahal Kenya, a top winning bitch in Europe and the United States. Handler is the late Roland Muller. Photo by Joan Ludwig.

Ch. Shirkhan of Grandeur, the 1957 Westminster Kennel Club best in show winner. This win marked the first time an Afghan Hound went all the way to top honors at this event, and the first time the winner was bred and shown by its owner. The striking, blue brindle, owned by Sunny Shay, continued to win best in show awards even past his tenth birthday.

Ch. Jui of Grandeur, a lovely blue bitch, whelped in May, 1957, was the first offspring of the renowned Ch. Shirkhan of Grandeur to finish her championship. Jui is owned by the Dale Henrys.

ben ghaZi kennels; and the author's Sahadi Kennels, to mention a few.

It was, and is, the integrity and foresight of such breeders as these that has helped advance and promote the Afghan Hound to the point we find it today. They have imported wisely, bred conscientiously, and exhibited and advertised widely to keep the Afghan Hound in the public eye and up to standard. Therefore, we could not consider a chapter on the history of the breed without mentioning some of the great dogs produced by these kennel owners, for they have earned their place in Afghan Hound history. We have already mentioned Ch. Badshah of Ainsdart, first Best In Show Afghan Hound in the USA, and we've mentioned Asra of Ghazni, Westmil Omar, Zahera, and International Champion Rudiki of Pride's Hill.

We must touch on the illustrious career of Ch. Turkuman Nissim's Laurel, imported by Sunny Shay and Sol Malkin from Mrs. Juliette de Bairacli-Levy. An American champion by 1947, the great "Kaftan" took the breed and the Hound Group at the Westminster Kennel Club Show in 1950 after having won the Afghan Hound Club of

America Specialty Show the day before the Garden event. Kaftan died of old age late in 1957 at Mrs. Shay's Grandeur Kennels after producing many excellent show puppies, top sires and show winners in their own right.

Another glorious hound that made a name for himself by winning two group firsts at Westminster, plus winning the Afghan Hound Club of America Specialty Show in 1954, is Ch. Taejon of Crown Crest, a black-masked silver, owned by Mrs. Kay Finch of Corona del Mar, California. "Johnny" was retired at the age of six, with nineteen Best In Show awards, four Specialty Show wins, forty-nine Hound Group firsts, and seventy-two Best of Breed wins. Johnny was undefeated in the breed for three consecutive years at all-breed

Int. Ch. Felt's Thief of Bagdad. This pale silver-blue male, pictured in a desert waste, was featured on the cover of the 1948 Christmas issue of Dog World Magazine. One of the foundation stud dogs in the Crown Crest Kennels, his name appears in many pedigrees of present day champions and show winners. Photo by Joan Ludwig.

Int. Ch. Crown Crest Zardonx arrives at Kennedy Airport, with owner Kay Finch, to repeat his best of breed win at the Afghan Hound Club of America Specialty Show in 1958.

The first Afghan Hound brace shown in this country: Ch. Meheronee Kahifafa and Int. Ch. Rudiki of Pride's Hill. Photo by William Brown.

shows from coast to coast, and was a favorite with the crowd wherever he was shown. His champion sons and daughters number in the thirties.

When speaking of Mrs. Finch's Crown Crest Kennels we must also mention her gorgeous black-masked red dog imported from Eva Pauptit's Oranje Manege Kennels in Holland. Ophaal was a champion in four countries: Germany, Belgium, Holland, and the United States. In three litters bred at Mrs. Finch's kennels, he sired two dozen champions. One of his sons, Crown Crest Zardonx, is himself an International Champion, having won the championship title in Mexico and Canada as well as the United States. At the time of his retirement in 1959 he had thirteen Best In Show awards, three Specialty Show wins, and fifty-seven Hound Group firsts on his record. Another of Ophaal's offspring who earned the International Champion title was Ch. Crown Crest Mr. Universe, who won his championship titles in Canada and the United States. While not shown as frequently today as he was in the early 1960's, his record consists of thirty-five Best In Show awards, four Specialty Show wins, and one hundred Hound Group firsts. This is the show winning record of all time in our breed. A great honor for a great Afghan Hound. "Mr. U' was co-owned by Charles Costabile of Las Vegas, Nevada, up until the time of Mr. Costabile's death. Owner Kay Finch now lists "Mr. U's" champion offspring in the twenties. This fabulous black-masked golden Afghan Hound was also runner-up for the Western Division of the Quaker Oats Award for the most group wins in the United States for the year 1959.

Mrs. Marjorie Lathrop's Majara Kennels has produced an unbroken line of six generations of Best In Show Afghan Hounds. Perhaps the greatest of these was Ch. Majara Mahabat, a Best In Show dog and a producer of fine show puppies. His son, Ch. Majara

Ch. Majara Mahabat, perhaps the greatest of the Afghan Hounds from Marjorie Lathrop's world-famous Majara Kennels. A best in show dog, and producer of fine show puppies, Mahabat has been one of the potent forces in the unbroken line of six generations of best in show winners bred at Majara. Tauskey Photo.

Ch. Crown Crest Taejhanne, dam of four champions in her first litter.
A daughter of the famous Ch. Taejon of Crown Crest, Taejhanne is
owned by H. G. Stephanson of the Patrician Kennels.

Ch. Kalli of Grandeur, only litter mate to Ch. Shirkhan of Grandeur. Kalli, a "typey" black bitch, finished her show career in short order, including a five point major win, and second only to her illustrious litter brother. Owned and shown by Joan Brearley.

Mihrab, was the winner of the parent club Specialty Show in 1953, the same show his father, Mahabat, had won in 1949 and co-won in 1948. Mihrab died in December of 1959, Mahabat in 1957. Their royal heritage dates back to the famous Ch. Badshah of Ainsdart.

Another Majara "great" was the lovely bitch Ch. Majara Mirza. Mirza, whose record is probably the greatest of all Afghan bitch records to date, was the winner of the Quaker Oats Award, Eastern Division, in 1951, for her record of nineteen Hound Group firsts. In her one and only litter, sired by Ch. Majara Mihrab, she produced five champions, including Ch. Majara Machiche, a Best In Show winner in Spain. Mirza was eleven years old when she died in December of 1959.

Mrs. Robert Tongren's ben ghaZi Kennels in Bloomfield, Connecticut produced the famous show and stud dog Ch. Karli ben ghaZi. Karli is the only dog ever to win the Afghan Hound Club of America

Specialty Show honors from the classes over specials competition. This remarkable win was made in 1952, under judge Alex Scott. As a champion, Karli won this show of shows again in 1955 under judge Eugene Beck. This same year he won the Potomac Afghan Hound Club Specialty Show as well. Karli has sired many champions, many of whom are making their mark in the show rings today.

Down through the years there have been many memorable Afghan Hounds of great beauty and near perfection. One such is Mr. and Mrs. Cyrus Rickel's Ch. Tanyah Sahib of Cy Ann, the Afghan Hound that judge Eugene Beck gave top honors at the Afghan Hound Club of America's very first Specialty Show, in 1940. Another was the beautiful Ch. Rajah of Arken, owned by Charles Wernsman, the only dog to win the Specialty Show three years in a row, 1942, 1943, and 1944. Others include Ch. Karach of Khanhasset and Ch. Karan of Khanhasset, owned by Leah P. McConaha; Ch. Blu Arabis of Kubera, owned by Howard and Lee Iverson; Ch. Hazar, owned by Dr. Gertrude Kinsey; and others including Sunny Shay and Dorothy Chenade's Ch. Shirkhan of Grandeur.

Ch. Crown Crest Mr. Universe, the greatest winning dog in the Afghan Hound breed, with thirty-five best in show wins, four specialty show wins and one hundred hound group firsts! "Mr. U." is a Canadian champion as well, and has over twenty champion sons and daughters winning at shows all over the United States.

Ch. Crown Crest Khalifah, one of the top producing bitches in the history of the breed, is the foundation bitch behind the author's Sahadi Kennels. Bred by Kay Finch, Khalifah has ten champions to her credit, with others pointed.

On February 12, 1957, in New York's Madison Square Garden, a shiny blue, two-and-a-half-year-old Afghan Hound took Best In Show honors over an entry of more than 2,500 dogs at America's top dog show, the Westminster Kennel Club. Ch. Shirkhan of Grandeur, co-owned by Sunny Shay and Dorothy Chenade, managed to set several records with his victory. Not only was the lovely Shirkhan the first Afghan Hound ever to win Best In Show at this event, but it was also the first time a hound had gone all the way to the top position at Westminster. Furthermore, it was the first time the handler of the dog was also the owner and the breeder.

While Afghan Hounds had been gaining steadily in breed registrations at the American Kennel Club, it was this big win at the Garden that brought the Afghan Hound to the attention of dog lovers the country over. New interest in the breed was created instantaneously, and show entries went up as well. While Afghan Hound breeders never wish to see their breed become overly popular, because indiscriminate breeding and selling eventually ruins the breed, it is

Ch. Tanjores Domino, imported by Mr. and Mrs. John Guzevich, earned his championship in Norway, Sweden, Finland, Austria, and then here in America, to make him the all-time championship title holder in the breed.

Int. Ch. Majara Mirza, one of the top winning bitches in the breed, with 19 hound group firsts. In her one and only litter, sired by Ch. Majara Mihrab, she produced 5 champions, including Ch. Majara Machiche, a best in show winner in Spain. Photo by William Brown.

believed that there are now many more Afghan Hound enthusiasts in this country who have the good of their dogs at heart than at any other time.

Ever since his victory at Westminster, Ch. Shirkhan of Grandeur has continued his winning streak. By 1964 he had over twenty-five Best In Show awards, almost a dozen Specialty Show wins and over one hundred Hound Group firsts. He celebrated his tenth birthday on August 10, 1964, and is still being shown and winning Best In Show honors! He is consistently winning and bringing thunderous applause from ringsiders whenever he steps into a show ring. Shirkhan is the living proof that truly great dogs get better as they get older.

Shirkhan's show record is even more commendable when you take his unusual color into consideration. This dark brindle color was never one of the most popular shades. While the standard for the breed clearly specifies that *any* color is acceptable, the most desired colors seem to be the fiery reds and the rich creams and silvers, with a black showing up now and again. But Shirkhan seems to have "broken the color line." We now see more and more of the rare colors in the show ring, which proves that a good dog looks good in any color.

An element of fate played a part in the show ring career of Shirkhan. Sunny Shay tells us that as a puppy Shirkhan had been sold to a young couple who wanted to buy foundation stock for

Ch. Jhaijhao Kawn Al Shaarq shown with breeder-owner Alma L. Wells on the right, and judge of the 1963 Afghan Hound Club of America Specialty Show, Kay Finch. Kawn is a black-masked golden daughter of the world-famous, Ch. Crown Crest Mr. Universe. Photo by Evelyn Shafer.

Ch. Taejon of Crown Crest, owned by Kay Finch, takes his third consecutive best of breed win at the Westminster Kennel Club. The year was 1954 and Taejon went on to capture his second consecutive hound group win at this same show. The judge was Haskell Schuffman. Photo by Evelyn Shafer.

breeding. Mrs. Shay was reluctant to part with the puppy, since she believed him to be a top show prospect. But since she still owned his sire, Ch. Blue Boy of Grandeur, she planned to repeat the breeding, and with this in mind, sold the dog to the young couple. Shortly after the puppy was sold, Blue Boy was killed while pushing one of Mrs. Shay's Poodles out from in front of the wheels of a speeding car. When, a few weeks after the fatal accident, the couple returned Shirkhan to Mrs. Shay because they had decided "he couldn't do any winning at the shows," she welcomed him back with open arms and now believes it an act of fate that Shirkhan had been returned to take the place of his father as a stud force and show winner for her Grandeur Kennels.

Space does not allow a listing of each and every newcomer and show-winning dog that has joined the ranks of Afghan Hounds in this country. But we can conclude that interest is increasing, for American Kennel Club registrations and show records are up more each year. One thing is certain: the prestige of the Afghan Hound and the quality of the hounds being shown in the show rings today is encouraging proof of a bright future for our breed in conformation competition, in the obedience ring, and in the world.!

THE AFGHAN HOUND IN AUSTRALIA

In yet another part of the world Afghan Hounds are increasing in popularity. Correspondence for some of the club bulletins from Norman Langdon of Australia reports that at least six Afghan Hounds

Ch. Alibaba of Scheherazade, English import bred and owned by Lt. Col. Wallace Pede. A Best In Show winner in England, Ali is now continuing his winning ways in the U.S.A.

Ch. LeGran Salaam de Grandeur owned by Diane and Frank La Greca. "Abba Dabba" is a group winner and a son of Ch. Shirkhan of Grandeur. He is shown here winning best of breed at the Lakes Region Kennel Club under judge Sadie Edmiston with Jane Kamp handling.

had been imported to Australia from England in 1963. Using the Royal Melbourne Show as a measuring stick, he states that in 1950 there were no Afghan Hound entries at a show that boasted almost 2,000 entrants.

Interest in the breed began to pick up in the show ring in 1957 with the usual one, two, or three entries that appeared starting in 1951, along with three new imports brought to Australia by an English couple transferred from Britain. Mr. Langdon purchased a

Ch. Kurram El Myia, (deceased) winner of four Canadian best in show awards and sixteen hound group firsts, was owned by Mary Matchett of the El Myia Kennels in Canada.

puppy from a breeding of two of the imports, which eventually became, and still is, the most outstanding Afghan Hound ever shown in Australia, Ch. Khyber Khorran, Challenge Winner at every Melbourne Royal Show since 1958, with one exception. He now has taken a Best In Show award in his stride. In 1963 Afghan Hound entries at this show reached twenty-seven; entries for following years are expected to top this figure easily.

The reason for the scarcity of American-bred dogs in Australia is that dogs from the United States must be shipped first to England for a six-month quarantine and then to Australia for an additional two-month quarantine. Obviously this makes the dog a good bit older and more expensive, with costs for transportation and quarantine running to nearly $500 over and above the original purchase price.

Ch. Majara Menelek, owned and bred by Mrs. Dixon Lathrop. "Minky" is one of an unbroken line of six generations of best in show dogs bred at Mrs. Lathrop's famous Majara Kennels.

A few Afghan Hound clubs with the good of the breed in mind are springing up "Down Under." Kenneth Cutbush is current president of the Afghan Hound Club of Queensland; there is an active club in South Australia, and the New South Wales Club has been in existence for three or four years.

Australians have even given Afghan Hound racing a try. In 1963 a club member's horse farm was the site for an experimental attempt. But, as elsewhere in the world, Australian racing beginners find the dogs more often interested in chasing each other, sniffing trees, or tracking down their owners than in pursuing the hare.

Ch. Crown Crest Rubi, a Best In Show dog and sire of many champions. He is owned by Ruth Tongren, and was bred by Kay Finch. Tauskey Photo.

NEW WORLDS TO CONQUER

In 1957, after Ch. Shirkhan of Grandeur won Best In Show at the Westminster Kennel Club Show, Mr. and Mrs. Harley Miller of Puerto Rico invited Sunny Shay to bring the now-famous dog to their island for exhibition.

Afghan Hounds were virtually unknown on the island and the Millers, who had come to admire the breed on visits to dog shows in this country, thought they would like dog fanciers in their club to see this great hound. Mrs. Shay responded, arriving with the blue brindle Afghan Hound and some other dogs that the Millers had purchased to help establish the breed on their island. The Afghan Hounds created quite a stir among dog owners in Puerto Rico, and soon the Millers were winning groups and Best In Show awards with their first Afghan Hound, Ch. Chinah of Grandeur.

The Millers have been very active in this breed ever since their original purchase and in 1963 finished to a championship their first home-bred Puerto Rican Afghan Hound, Ch. Harleana's Mukhalla El Wahid. The Millers have given a great deal of effort to the promotion of the breed and have been given much publicity in the newspapers with full pages of pictures of these exotic dogs.

Mr. Miller is not only President of the Puerto Rican Kennel Club but is also Puerto Rican columnist for *Popular Dogs* magazine in the territory, reporting on all breeds of dogs on the island.

Chapter III
The Afghan Hound in Art

From the days when hieroglyphics were first etched on the walls of Egypt's tombs and scratched across papyrus with quills from ancient desert birds, slender dogs resembling our Afghan Hound have been part of recorded history. Because of the great beauty of these fleetfooted hunters and guard dogs, they have managed to capture the eye of artists and art lovers down through the passing centuries. Through artistic endeavors on tombstones, papyrus, frescoes on flat stones, woodcuts, carvings, sculptures, oil paintings, the general press, and modern day ceramics and art mediums we have been able to enjoy the Afghan Hound in all its splendor.

Back in the early part of this century, when Afghan Hounds were first imported to England, the symmetry of this graceful, unusual dog came to the attention of the British artist Frederick T. Daws. Perhaps the first to do oil paintings of the Afghan Hound greats, Mr. Daws' works, which are of considerable size and great accuracy, have become collectors' items among fanciers in our breed.

Marion Foster Florsheim brought several to this country years ago, one of which she later sold to Kay Finch. A beautiful mountain tor setting for four of the all-time Afghan Hound greats, Ch. Westmil Omar, Ch. Badshah of Ainsdart, Ch. Sirdar of Ghazni, and Ch. Azri-Havid of Ghazni, it quite properly occupies a prominent location in Mrs. Finch's livingroom. Mrs. Florsheim came into possession of a number of Daws' paintings upon the death of her good friend Phyllis Robson of England. Mrs. Florsheim has expressed intentions of donating these recent acquisitions to the American Kennel Club.

But the artist who has done more to immortalize the Afghan Hound in our time, bar none, is Kay Finch herself. As an owner, breeder, and judge of many of the country's best and most beautiful Afghan Hounds in the history of the breed, Mrs. Finch has managed to

In 1956 Kay Finch, prominent artist and ceramist, created this fabric design in her California studios. It was a popular fashion item, made up into skirts and dresses, but also as drapery, towel and hanky items that were sometimes used as bench decorations at dog shows.

capture the true conformation and personality of this distinctive hound in her art forms.

Mrs. Finch's California studio has produced replicas of several of our great dogs in ceramics and other art media, including fabrics and statuary, that have been sold all over this country and in twenty-one foreign lands as well. She has produced both serious and comical studies of our lovely dogs in the form of ash trays, steins, plates, lamp bases, toweling and draperies, and bench decorations at the dog shows. Her head studies and full figure models have adorned trophies presented at our best and biggest dog shows. It is not uncommon at the same dog shows that present Mrs. Finch's art works as trophies to see Mrs. Finch make an entrance into the show ring with one of her beautiful Afghan Hounds whose likeness has been painted in exotic colors on her skirt!

Perhaps the most famous of Mrs. Finch's designs is the full figure bronze she created of Int. Ch. Rudiki of Pride's Hill. Another is the classic head study she presented to Sunny Shay and Sol Malkin after their exotic black imported dog, Ch. Turkuman Nissim's Laurel, won the Afghan Hound Club of America Specialty Show and the Hound Group at the Westminster Kennel Club show in 1950.

As our breed becomes increasingly popular, more and more artists are beginning to try to present this unusual dog in various art forms. Its likeness now appears, it seems, on everything from dish towels to note paper. And adorned with sprigs of holly or bedecked with wreaths, Afghan Hounds show up on countless Christmas cards each year in increasing numbers. Two Afghan Hound owners who

The championship medals awarded at the Wiesbaden, Germany show offer an indication of the importance of the Afghan Hound to continental exhibitors.

are artists by trade are now donating oil paintings as trophies at our dog shows. Mary Nelson Stephenson is well known for her magnificent oil and water color paintings of our breed, and Elizabeth Harvey Treharne is noted for her note paper and art work on various forms of glassware.

In Weisbaden, Germany, one of the medals awarded for championship, called the "Certificate of Aptitude for Championship of International Beauty," features head studies of a Great Dane and an

As part of an agricultural fair, the Government of Afghanistan issued this commemorative stamp. It clearly depicts an Afghan Hound, and also indicated the importance of the breed in his own country.

Afghan Hound. In Afghanistan, a stamp has been issued featuring a full figure of the Afghan Hound; the face value of the stamp is two pouls. The subtitle is *Postes Afghanes*, which identifies the stamp's country of origin, and the commemoration marks the Afghan Hound's part in an agricultural fair.

The most unique presentation of the Afghan Hound in recent years, however, is an exquisitely tooled Afghan Hound on a large natural leather handbag which Mrs. Kay Finch carried on her travels all through Europe in 1963 and had autographed by Afghan Hound owners and exhibitors all over Europe and the United States.

This magnificient, wind-blown headstudy of American and Mexican Ch. Crown Crest Zardonx, was featured on one of breeder-owner Kay Finch's Christmas cards. "Zar" won best of breed at the Afghan Hound Club of America's Specialty Show in 1957 under judge Mrs. Lauer Froelich, and repeated the win the following year under judge Anna Katherine Nicholas. Photo by Joan Ludwig.

Chapter IV
Standard for the Afghan Hound

Submitted by the Afghan Hound Club of America
Approved by the American Kennel Club, September 1948

THE STANDARD

General Appearance:

The Afghan Hound is an aristocrat, his whole appearance one of dignity and aloofness with no trace of plainness or coarseness. He has

Ch. Karli ben ghaZi was the only Afghan Hound to win best of breed at the Afghan Hound Club of America specialty show from the classes before attaining him championship. Karli was co-owned by Ruth Tongren and Josephine Baird. Photo by William Brown.

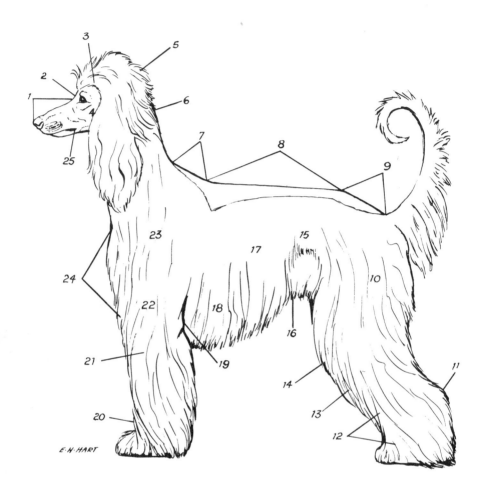

1. Foreface (including muzzle). 2. Stop. 3. Skull. 4. Cheek. 5. Occiput.
6. Crest of neck. 7. Withers. 8. Back (or saddle). 9. Croup. 10. Thigh.
11. Joint of hock. 12. Metatarsus (front of hock). 13. Lower thigh.
14. Stifle joint (knee). 15. Loin. 16. Tuck up (abdomen). 17. Ribs.
18. Brisket. 19. Elbow. 20. Pastern. 21. Forearm. 22. Upper arm.
23. Shoulder blade. 24. Forechest. 25. Lip corner (flew).

a straight front, proudly carried head, eyes gazing into the distance as if in memory of ages past. The striking characteristics of the breed—exotic or "Eastern" expression, long silky topknot, peculiar coat pattern, very prominent hip bones, large feet, and the impression of a somewhat exaggerated bend in the stifle due to profuse trouserings —stand out clearly, giving the Afghan Hound the appearance of what he is, a King of Dogs, that has held true to tradition throughout the ages.

Ch. Crown Crest Kabul, a best in show and specialty show winner, sired by the famous Int. Ch. Ophaal of Crown Crest, out of Ch. Crown Crest Taejoan. Bred by Kay Finch, Kabul is owned by Mary Nelson Stephenson.

Canadian and American Ch. Khubsurat Kahn, best in show winner in Canada, is owned by Mary Matchett.

Head:

The head is of good length showing much refinement, the skull evenly balanced with the foreface. There is a slight prominence of the nasal bone structure causing a slight Roman appearance, the center line running up over the foreface with little or no stop, falling away in front of the eyes so there is an absolutely clear outlook with no interference; the underjaw showing great strength, the jaws long and punishing; the mouth level, meaning that the teeth from the upper jaw and lower jaw match evenly neither overshot nor undershot. (This is a difficult mouth to breed. A scissors bite is even more punishing and can be more easily bred into a dog than a level mouth, and a dog having a scissors bite, where the lower teeth slip inside and rest against the teeth of the upper jaw, should not be penalized.) The occipital bone is very prominent. The head is surrounded by a topknot of long, silky hair.

Ears:

The ears are long, set approximately on level with outer corners of the eyes, the leather of the ear reaching nearly to the end of the dog's nose, and covered with long, silky hair.

Another perfect headstudy of an Afghan Hound. Ch. Sahadi Sadruddin, a black-masked golden son of the famous Ch. Taejon of Crown Crest out of Ch. Crown Crest Khalifah.

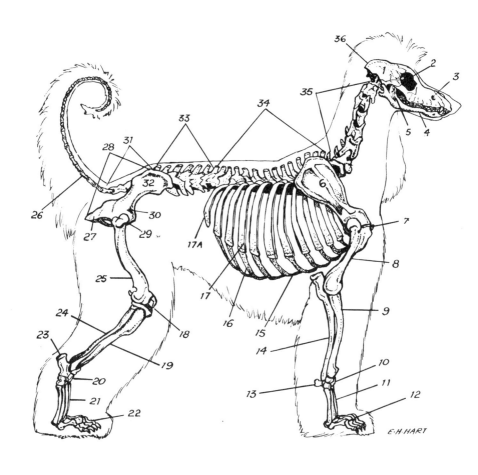

1. Cranium (skull). 2. Orbital cavity. 3. Nasal Bone. 4. Mandible (lower jaw). 5. Condyle. 6. Scapula (shoulder blade). 7. Prosternum (front end of sternum). 8. Humerus (upper arm). 9. Radius (front forearm bone). 10. Carpus (pastern joint). 11. Metacarpus (pastern). 12. Phalanges (toes). 13. Disiform. 14. Ulna. 15. Sternum. 16. Costal cartilage. 17. Rib bones. 17A. Floating rib. 18. Patella (knee joint or stifle). 19. Tibia. 20. Tarsus. 21. Metatarsus. 22. Phalanges. 23. Os calcis (point of hock). 24. Fibula. 25. Femur (thigh bone). 26. Coccygeal vertebra (tail bones). 27. Pubis. 28. Pelvic bone entire. 29. Head of femur. 30. Ischium. 31. Sacral vertebra. 32. Illium. 33. Lumbar vertebra. 34. Thoracic vertebra. 35. Cervical vertebra (.bones of neck). 36. Occiput.

Eyes:

The eyes are almond shaped (almost triangular), never full or bulgy, and they are dark in color.

Nose:

The nose is of good size, black in color.

FAULTS: Coarseness; snipiness; overshot or undershot; eyes round or lacking substance.

Body:

The back line appears practically level from the shoulders to the loin, strong and powerful loin and slightly arched, falling away toward the stern, with the hip bones very pronounced; well ribbed and tucked up in flanks. The height at the shoulders equals the distance from the chest to the buttocks; the brisket well let down and of medium width.

FAULTS: Roach back; sway back; goose rump; slack loin; lack of prominence of hip bones; too much width of brisket causing interference with elbows.

A headstudy of Ch. Zaamarakuri of Ghazni, a best in show sire of a best in show son, Ch. Hassan Ben of Moornistan. Kuri is owned by Mary Kenney.

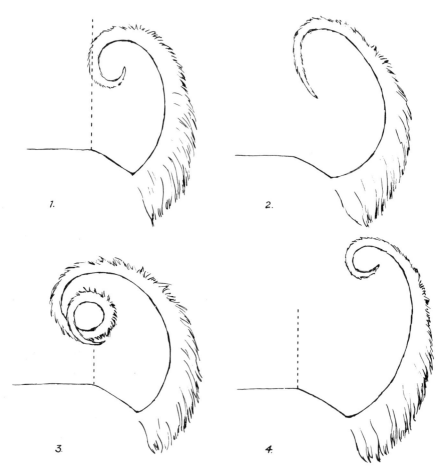

1. Proper tail carriage, erect and in line with hip bones.
2. Faulty, curved tail.
3. Undesirable double ring. Also carried too far over back.
4. Not in line with hip bones, long and with ring at end. Undesirable.

Tail:

The tail is set not too high on the body, having a ring or a curve on the end. It should never be curled over, or rest on the back, or be carried sideways, and is never bushy.

Legs:

The forelegs are straight and strong with great length between elbow and pastern; elbows well held in; forefeet large in both length and width; toes well arched; feet covered with long, thick hair, fine in texture; pasterns long and straight; pads of feet unusually large and well down on the ground. Shoulders have plenty of angulation so that the legs are well set underneath the dog. Too much straightness of shoulder causes the dog to break down in the pasterns, and this is a serious fault.

All four feet of the Afghan Hound are in line with the body, turning neither in nor out. The hind feet are broad and of good length; the toes arched, and covered with long, thick hair; hindquarters powerful and well muscled with great length between hip and hock; hocks are well let down; good angulation of both stifle and hock; slightly bowed from hock to crotch.

FAULTS: Front or back feet thrown outward or inward; pads of feet not thick enough; feet too small; or any other evidence of weakness in the feet; weak or broken down pasterns; too straight in stifle; too long in hock.

Coat:

Hindquarters, flanks, ribs, forequarters and legs are well covered with thick, silky hair, very fine in texture; ears and all four feet well feathered. From in front of the shoulders, and also backwards from

1. Desired level bite
2. Acceptable scissors bite
3. Overshot Undesirable
4. Undershot Undesirable

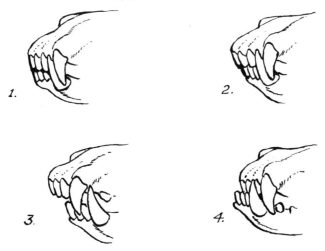

A lovely headstudy of Kalah, owned by Jay and Blair Nelson.

the shoulders along the saddle from the flanks and ribs upwards, the hair is short and close, forming a smooth back in mature dogs—this is a traditional characteristic of the Afghan Hound.

The Afghan Hound is shown in its natural state; the coat is not clipped or trimmed; the head is surmounted (in the full sense of the word) with a topknot of long, silky hair—this also an outstanding characteristic of the Afghan Hound. Showing of short hair on cuffs on either front or back legs is permissible.

FAULTS: Lack of short haired saddle in mature dogs.

Height:

Dogs, 27 inches, plus or minus one inch.

Bitches, 25 inches, plus or minus one inch.

Weight:

Dogs, about sixty pounds.

Bitches, about fifty pounds.

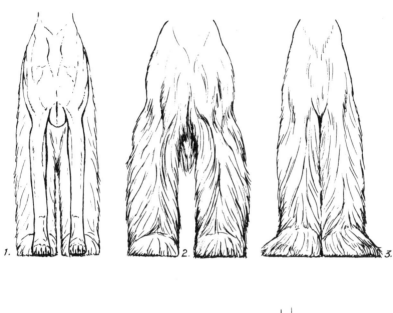

1. Excellent front, showing proper conformation hidden by coat.
2. Loaded in shoulder, too wide, legs set too far apart. 3. Narrow, shelly, feet "east and west" (pointing out), ebows pinched in.

1. Excellent rear, showing proper conformation hidden by coat.
2. Faulty rear. Cowhocked.

Color:

All colors are permissible, but color or color combinations are pleasing. White markings, especially on the head, are undesirable.

Gait:

When running free, the Afghan Hound moves at a gallop, showing great elasticity and spring in his smooth, powerful stride.

When on a loose lead, the Afghan can trot at a fast pace. Stepping along, he has the appearance of placing the hind feet directly in the foot prints of the front feet, both thrown straight ahead. Moving with head and tail high, the whole appearance of the Afghan Hound is one of great style and beauty.

Temperament:

Aloof and dignified, yet gay.

FAULTS: Sharpness or shyness.

SPECIAL CONSIDERATIONS

A dog show judge or a veterinarian will always examine your dog's teeth, and especially check his bite. There are forty-two permanent teeth, twenty on top and twenty-two on the lower jaw. Our standard calls for a level mouth, with a level bite. But a scissors bite is also acceptable. A badly overshot or undershot bite is undesirable.

Needless to say, your dog's teeth should be kept clean. Pet shops sell the proper instruments for doing this, or, in more severe cases, your veterinarian can do it. Dog biscuits are a great help in keeping teeth clean and free of tartar. When breeding your dog, be sure to check the bite of the stud or bitch, since a bad bite is very difficult to "breed out" once it shows up in your bloodlines.

One of the most beautiful and unusual characteristics of the Afghan Hound is the tail. It is not set too high on the body and must be carried erect when the dog is in motion. There is a ring or curve at the end, and the tail should not be bushy or touch down on the dog's back.

Chapter V
Buying Your
Afghan Hound Puppy

There are several trails that will lead you to a litter of puppies where you can find the Afghan Hound of your choice. There are the classified columns in the newspaper and your dog magazines. Or you might attend a dog show and locate a kennel through the advertisements in the show catalogue. You would also do well to telephone or write the American Kennel Club in New York City (51 Madison Ave., N.Y.C., N.Y.) and request the name and address of the secretary of the Afghan Hound Club of America. The secretary will be happy to put you in touch with club members who have puppies for sale. Although pet shops do not normally carry stocks of so select

A family portrait of ten-week-old future best in show winners. This "Jubilee Litter," sired by American and Canadian Ch. Felt's Thief of Bagdad, was the first litter born at Kay Finch's now famous Crown Crest Kennels.

a dog as the Afghan Hound, pet shop proprietors often can direct a prospective purchaser to a reputable breeder.

Once you've chosen the Afghan Hound as your breed because you admire its exceptional beauty, intelligence, and personality and because you feel the Afghan Hound will fit in with your family's way of life, it is wise to read as much literature as possible on the breed. Any library, bookshop, or pet shop can get hold of this information for you. When you have gone over this background material, it is time to start writing letters and making phone calls and appointments to see puppies.

A word of caution: don't let your choice of a kennel be determined by its nearness to your home, and then buy the first "cute" puppy that romps across your instep or licks the end of your nose. All puppies are cute, and naturally you'll have a preference among those you see. But don't let preferences sway you. If you are buying your

A mother and daughter siesta at Charles Farley's Kumar Kennels. Proud and protective mother is Ami of Kumar; slightly demure daughter is Kala of Kumar.

Ameer of Scheherezade, pictured at six weeks of age, is owned by the Zoltan Glass Company of France and London, England. Sire is Lt. Col. Wallace Pede's Ch. Bletchingley Ragman of Scheherezade.

Afghan Hound as a family pet, preferences are permissible. But if you are looking for a quality puppy with show prospects, you must think clearly, choose wisely, and make the best possible choice. You will learn to love your Afghan Hound, whichever one you choose, whereas a case of "love at first sight" can be disappointing later on.

To get the broadest possible concept of what is for sale and the current market prices, it is recommended that you visit as many kennels as possible in your area and write to others farther away. With today's safe and rapid air cargo flights on the major airlines, it is possible to secure dogs from far-off places at nominal costs. While it is always safest and wisest to see the dog you are buying, there are enough reputable breeders and kennels to be found for you to take this step with a minimum of risk. It can be well worth your while to obtain the exact dog or bloodline you desire. It is customary for the purchaser to pay the shipping charges, and the airlines are most willing to supply flight information and prices upon request. Rental on the shipping crate is also low.

Sadi, a rare blue. She is owned and was bred by the Hewitts.

Kay Finch gets in some early show training with Crown Crest Kaejorg, a two-month-old son of the great Taejon. This puppy was later sent to Stockholm, Sweden for a show career. This was the first Afghan Hound export to Sweden. Photo by Joan Ludwig.

WHAT TO LOOK FOR IN AN AFGHAN PUPPY

In few other breeds would you find the young puppy so different from the adult dog. Other breeds such as Dalmatians, Pointers, Ascob Cockers, Harlequin Danes, etc., have their colors and markings pretty well established at birth. They are recognizable as puppies of their specific breed. But it has been said of the Afghan Hound puppy that to the uneducated eye it resembles a smooth-coated cross between a Cocker Spaniel and a Collie, but certainly not the silky-coated, glamorous Afghan Hound it grows up to be.

For those who have seen Afghan Hound puppies this comes as no surprise. One of the most fascinating aspects of raising an Afghan Hound is experiencing the extraordinary and complete metamorphosis that occurs during the first year of life. Despite this marked change in appearance there are certain qualities you must look for in the puppy that will generally make for a good adult dog. Of course, no one can guarantee nature, and the best puppy does not always grow up to be a top dog. But even the neophyte prospective buyer can learn to look for certain specifics that will help him choose a promising puppy.

Let us assume you are going to buy a two-to-three-month-old puppy. This is about the age when a puppy is weaned, wormed, and ready to go out into the world with his new owner. Perhaps even before you notice much about his appearance you will observe his

"Three little Afghan Hounds that made good" is the title the breeder of these puppies gave this photograph. They all grew up to be champions. Ch. Ivardon Iokanaan, Ch. Zambars Zachariah, and Ch. Zambars Jabez. Ch. Ivardon Salome, their dam, is pictured with them. These dogs were bred by Mr. and Mrs. Sam Magill.

Ouijah of Al-Yram, owned by Joan Brearley. The breeder is Roberta Breath. Ouijah is a daughter of Ch. Sahadi Sinbad. Photo by William Gilbert.

behavior. Puppies, as they are recalled in our fondest memories, are quite gay and active, as well they should be. The puppy should be interested, alert, and quite curious, especially about a stranger. If a puppy acts a little strange or distant, this need not be misconstrued as shyness or fear. He just hasn't made up his mind if he likes you. But he should not be fearful or terrified by you or his owner.

In direct contrast, he should not be overly active either. The puppy that frantically bounds around the room and is never still is not particularly desirable either. And beware of spinners! These are dogs or puppies that have become neurotic from being kept in cramped quarters or in crates all the time. When released at last, they run in circles and behave in a most emotionally unstable manner. The dog that has had the proper exercise and appropriate, comfortable living quarters will have a normal, spirited outlook on life and will do his utmost to win you over without having to go into a tailspin.

If the general behavior and appearance of the dog appeals to you, it is time for you to observe him more closely for his physical attributes. First of all, you can't expect to find the long coat that the adult dog acquires. Puppies have a short, velvety coat that should have a lovely shine to it. Naturally, the thicker the coat the better.

AKC COVER — Two glorious Afghan Hounds featured on the February 1957 issue of the American Kennel Gazette magazine. This notable publication, Pure-Bred Dogs, is considered the "Bible" of the dog world.

Ch. Crown Crest Camelot, pictured at 7 months of age, winning reserve dog at the Santa Barbara Kennel Club under judge Bea Godsol. Owned and bred by Kay Finch, Camelot's sire is Ch. Sahadi Shikari, his dam is Ch. Crown Crest Hi-Bhutiphaal. Photo by Joan Ludwig.

Look for clear, dark, sparkling eyes, free of discharge. Dark eye rims or lids are most desirable and should be small and almond shaped. From the time the puppy's eyes open until the puppy is about three months old the eyes might have a slightly blue cast to them. The darker the blue the better the chances are for a good dark eye in the adult dog. They should slant upwards at the outer corners and not set too far apart. The head is not too domed, with a strong indication, even at this age, of a long, lean muzzle.

Check the bite. Even though the puppy will get another complete set of teeth somewhere between four and seven months of age, there will be some indication of their final position. You don't want too much of an overshot bite (top teeth too far out over the bottom teeth) or a badly undershot jaw (bottom teeth too far out under the top teeth). The gums should be pink in color, and the teeth should be a clear, clean white.

Ch. Kheiba of Tajmir, owned by the Soroya Kennels of Mr. and Mrs.
E. F. Winter. Kheiba was bred by Patricia Sinden, and sired by Ch.
Karli ben ghaZi out of Ch. Crown Crest Khitiiku, C.D. She is the dam
of several champion offspring.

A litter of puppies from Stormhill Kennels. These future champions line up for inspection. Photo by Joan Ludwig.

Afghan Hound Puppies undergo a tremendous change before reaching maturity. Proper care, feeding, and management will help these youngsters emerge as the elegant animals they will grow into. Photo by Three Lions.

Puppies take anything and almost everything into their mouths to chew on, and a lot of diseases and infections start, or are introduced in this area. Brown-stained teeth, for instance, may indicate a past or present case of distemper, and they will stay that way. This must be reckoned with if you have a show puppy in mind. The puppy's breath should not be sour or unpleasant. This can be a result of a poor mixture of food in the diet, or too low quality of meat, especially if fed raw. Some say the healthy puppy's breath has a faint odor vaguely reminiscent of garlic.

Ears should be well furred, with the leather reaching to the end of the nose. There is little or no topknot at this age and there is no saddle, perhaps only the suggestion of a shade of color down the middle of the back. The feet should be exceptionally large, with thick pads, and little wisps of fur should be beginning to show between the toes.

Ch. Kauno Lavas, owned, and handled by Joan Stepanauckas. This import has excelled in the showring and the race track. The Best of Winners dog at the Afghan Hound Club of America Specialty Show in New York in 1964, Lavas has won in Austria, France, Italy, Germany, and Switzerland and has silver medals for racing wins at Landeisieger and Hamburg, Germany. Now being shown as an American champion, Lavas has two hound group firsts to date. Photo by Stephen Klein.

Kharontule Mystique owned by Mel McCarthy and Nancy McCarthy Gardner. Misty is a replica of her dam, Ch. Sahadi Sequin.

The impression should be that this puppy is a true hound. This means that the dog should have great depth of brisket, with good tuck-up and long, slender legs. The topline should be level, and the puppy should have great reach of neck. The hip bones are prominent even at this young age, and the tail should not be set too high on the body. The front legs should be straight down from the shoulders and well under the body, and the rear legs should be well angulated and in a line directly behind the front legs. The general appearance of the puppy when viewed from the side should be "squarish."

The final form of an Afghan Hound's tail is difficult to predict while the dog is still a puppy. While it is almost impossible to expect the strong erect tail carriage of the grown dog in a puppy, there should be a definite indication to curl or at least curve into the desired ring at the end. If there is a curl at this age, so much the better! The tail is not yet feathered and should never curve up over the body and touch down onto the back. When stretched out to its full length it should reach down at least to the hocks.

Needless to say, the puppy should be clean. The breeder that shows a dirty puppy is one to steer away from! Look closely at the skin. Make sure it is not covered with insect bites or red, blotchy sores or dry scales. The vent area about the tail should not show evidences of diarrhea or inflammation. By the same token, the puppy's fur should not be matted with excretion or smell strongly of urine. True

A family portrait of Kay Finch and the dam and sire of one of the "winningest" litters ever bred. The famous Gem Litter was sired by the famous import, American, Dutch, Belgian and German Ch. Ophaal of Crown Crest. The dam is Ch. Crown Crest Taejoan. This Gem Litter included Int. Ch. Crown Crest Zardonx, Ch. Crown Crest Rubi, Ch. Crown Crest Topaz, Ch. Crown Crest Dhi-mond. Photo by Joan Ludwig.

Ch. Crown Crest Devikkrakit poses after winning a hound group before his retirement from the showring. Owner Gertrude Curnyn then launched him on his racing career. Photo by William Brown.

enough, you can wipe dirty eyes, clean dirty ears, and give the puppy a bath when you get it home, but these are all indications of how the puppy has been cared for during the important formative first months of its life, and can influence its health and future development. There are many healthy puppies for sale that have been brought up in clean kennels or private homes, so why take a chance on a series of vet bills unnecessarily?

The color of your Afghan Hound is a matter of your own preference, as are the contrasting colors on the ears and mask. Black on the muzzle and ear fringes is referred to as the "points." Puppies may be born with white feet or tail tips, but they usually blend in; however, if you intend to show your dog in the breed ring, white on the face is most undesirable. The choice of sex is also a matter of your personal choice, but even at this young age, if you purchase a male, make sure you or your veterinarian determines the presence of both testicles. Having only one descended testicle (monorchidism) will automatically disqualify your dog from the show ring and make him less desirable as a stud dog; having no visible testicles will, of course, bar the dog from the show ring.

You must not be afraid to ask pertinent questions about the puppy you intend to buy. Feel free to ask the breeder if you might see the dam (to establish her general health and appearance as a representative of the breed), ask what the puppy has been fed and

This intimate candid shot of Ch. Kora, bred by the Baroness de Rothchild, and owned by Karen and Julian Armistead, shows the comical side of Afghan Hounds. Delighted to pose for this mischievous shot, Kora's breeder and owners acclaim her illustrious parentage in her sire, Vaz's Grey Gregor, and her dam Eline von Wassenaar, an Austrian import.

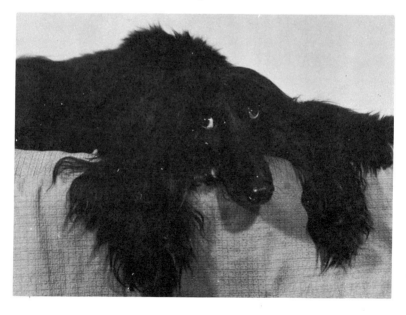

Sahadi Shawnee Pocahontis, foundation brood bitch for the Kharon-tule Kennels. Shawnee was bred by Joan Brearley. Sire: Ch. Crown. Crest Jesi Jhaimz; dam: Ch. Crown Crest Khalifah.

should be fed, ask to see the pedigree, inquire if either the litter or the individual puppy has been registered with the American Kennel Club, how many of the temporary and permanent inoculations the puppy has had, when and if he has been wormed, and if he's had any serious illnesses or infections. For your own convenience you might also ask if the puppy has been housebroken. But do not expect too much of him. He may know where the "spot" is in the house where he now lives, but he will have to learn where you want the "spot" to be in your house!

A reputable, sincere breeder will welcome these questions and voluntarily offer additional information, if only to "brag" about the conscientious care he has given his dog's offspring! A reputable breeder will sell a puppy on twenty-four-hour veterinarian approval, and also should present you with veterinary certificates with full information on the dates and kinds of inoculations the puppy has had to date. The vet will also be able to tell you about the general condition of the puppy and advise you on the possible presence of worms.

We must give further attention to the subject of worms in puppies at this point. Generally speaking, all puppies, even puppies reared in clean quarters, come into contact with worms early in life. To say that one must not buy a particular puppy because it has worms might mean passing up a quality dog. Worming has become a relatively minor ailment if caught in the early stages and treated properly. It is up to your vet to determine how heavily infested the puppy is, the amount of dosage to be administered, and whether or not the dog's general condition has been harmed in any way.

When your veterinarian is going over your puppy you might as well ask him his opinion of it. Most veterinarians have a good eye for an all-round good specimen, although they might not be familiar with all the finer points required in each breed. But he can point out

Ch. Khabiri of Grandeur, owned by Werner (and handler) Jennifer Sheldon wins best in show honors at the Lackawanna Kennel Club under judge W. F. Gilroy. "Lance" is the sire of the Best In Show winning dog, Ch. Holly Hill Desert Wind. Photo by Evelyn Shafer.

Ch. Siah Nayd of Shahi-Taj, owned by William Walsh, is many times a group winner.

the serious faults that apply to all dogs, such as whether or not the puppy is cow-hocked or roach-backed, or has a broken tail, poor eye color, etc., in addition to informing you of its general health.

It is customary for you to pay for the puppy before you take it away with you. If there is a doubt in your mind as to the health of the puppy, you might suggest post-dating a check to cover you on the twenty-four-hour veterinarian approval. If you keep the puppy the breeder is required to send you the certificate of ownership promptly upon cashing your check. This you will sign and send with $1 to the American Kennel Club to transfer ownership of the dog over into your name.

Many breeders, especially those with the more expensive breeds, will offer customers time payment plans for buying convenience. These terms must be worked out individually between buyer and seller. You will find most breeders to be cooperative if they believe you are sincere in your love for the puppy and will give it the proper home.

Chapter VI

Grooming the Afghan Hound

GROOMING METHODS AND EQUIPMENT

All dogs, but particularly long-coated dogs such as the Afghan Hound, require good grooming. A beautifully-coated dog which wears proudly the thick, silky coat you've taken time and trouble to cultivate is a joy to behold, both in and out of the show ring. Once ruined, or cut off, the coat of the Afghan Hound requires two years'

Ch. Crown Rubi, winner of three best in show awards, is owned by the ben ghaZi Kennels. Rubi is from Kay Finch's Gem Litter, and was bred at her Crown Crest Kennels. Photo by Evelyn Shafer.

103

Original Afghan Hound grooming chart, conceived and created by the author.

Arrows indicate direction in which Afghan coat should be combed.

time and daily care to come to its original length and luster. Therefore it is wise to take a little time each day to keep it in top condition rather than have to work diligently on the dog for a couple of days if he's to be presented in the show ring.

To establish grooming as a common practice in the daily routine, you'll find matters simplified by choosing a particular spot for grooming your dog each time. Place the grooming table where the light is good and where the dog will have reasonably few distractions. Eliminate temptations by keeping toys, food, other dogs, etc., out of sight. Make the dog know there is work to be done and that you mean to do it. Be firm (but gentle) about it.

As soon as the dog is capable of jumping up onto the table, encourage him to do so. Give him the command to "stand" so it becomes clear that the time for grooming has come. How you choose to position your dog while grooming is not merely a matter of choice

Ch. Patterson's Artemis, beautifully coated, black-masked red bitch owned by Mrs. Donald Patterson. Artemis was winner bitch at the Westminster Kennel Club show in 1964.

or convenience. To groom thoroughly you will find you will have to have him both standing and reclining on each side. Since the most difficult areas to work on are the underside, the most practical start is on the one side first and then the other. Stand the dog up long enough, however, to get his footing on the table, and at the end of the grooming session for the rest of the grooming and the finishing touches.

Make sure the table you use is sturdy. Don't use one that tips from side to side. Dogs are comfortable only when they are sure of their footing. As for the height of the table, make it easy for yourself. In the areas where you will be doing the most work you will not want to reach up or down too far. So set the height at your convenience, and the narrower the better. Make the surface rough enough for the dog to get a good grip with his feet, yet smooth enough to be wiped off easily after each use.

Mrs. William Waskow and one of the Afghan Hounds from her Little Fir Kennels pose in front of the Wisconson State Capitol building in their Afghan coats. Mrs. Waskow's coat is made from hair from her Afghan Hounds, and was carded, spun, woven, cut and sewn by a friend. Afghan hair has been used for sweaters, but this is the first time it has been made into a coat.

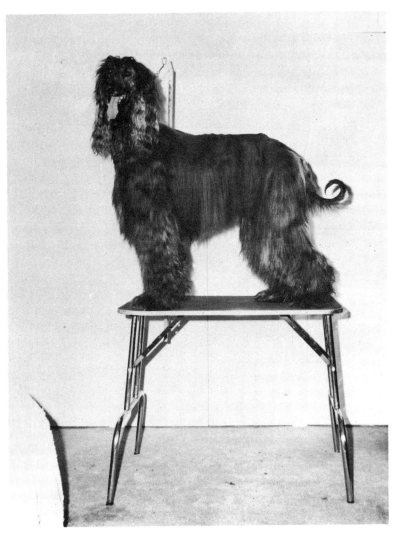

If you show dogs — or even for your own convenience at home — it is almost essential that you have a sturdy grooming table and pole with slip lead to groom your dog properly. The grooming table shown above is covered with ribbed rubber matting to assure steady footing and the pole is adjustable to each individual dog's height. It should be high enough to keep the head up and yet not so high that it chokes him if he moves a little from one side to another during the grooming session. The table, set up in the center of the room allows you to groom all of the dog by walking around the table without having to lean over or bending to reach the lower portions of the dog.

There is no set amount of time recommended for grooming. Dogs that are more heavily coated will naturally require more grooming time. But enough time should be allotted for going over the entire dog each time it is put up on the table. What you skip over one time will be twice as hard to remedy the next time. The spots you miss will show up all too soon!

The correct brush for the Afghan Hound should have soft bristles, not nylon! The hair should be brushed in layers from the skin out to the very ends of the hair. If your brush is gathering hair on one side only, you are not holding it correctly. The strokes should be gentle, and the entire stroke should be straight, with no twist of the wrist. It is usually easier to start on the legs, working up to the body, holding the layers of hair up with one hand and the flat of your arm while brushing with the other hand. As time goes by you will develop your own pattern for grooming, deciding where to start and finish to make it easier for you and your dog.

Giving medication to a dog can be simple if properly done. Here is the proper technique for preparing to open the mouth. Place fingers over muzzle and use your thumb to open jaws, and then place thumb on roof of mouth. With the other hand support the lower jaw, until mouth is open fully. Using thumb and forefinger, place pill down throat at rear corner of mouth on the side nearest you.

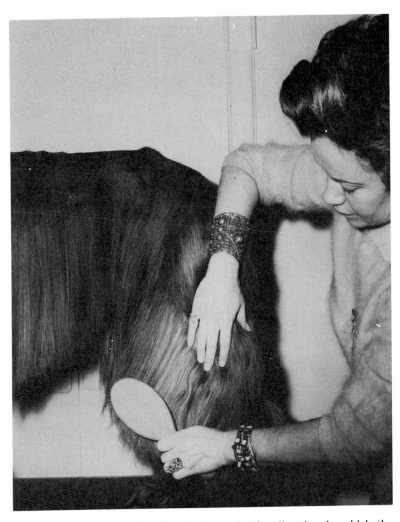

Here the coat is being brushed in layers in the direction in which the coat is to fall. Notice also that the brush is used flat against the dog's body with no "twist of the wrist" motion.

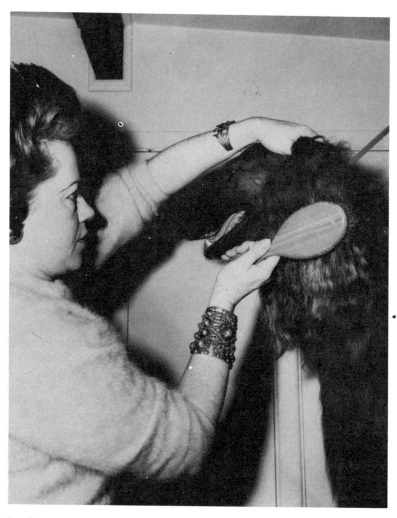

Brushing the ears can be done in layers as well as "fluffed up." Be sure not to forget the inside of the ear! Reverse the ear and lay the leather down against the length of neck and brush gently. After the ears are completely brushed out, they should be brushed downward once again. Use caution in grooming your dog's head. Make sure the brush stays away from his eyes.

For the most part, the brushing should be done with the lay of the hair. With puppies it is stimulating to the skin and the hair for it to be brushed directly opposite at times. Since you are dealing with puppy coat, this "going against the grain" does the hair no serious harm and stimulates the hair cells to encourage growth of permanent coat.

The head should be brushed both up and back and then down forward over the eyes. This wild appearance of the topknot is characteristic of the Afghan Hound. The ears require considerable brushing. This is one of the major tangle areas. The inside of the ears can best be brushed by laying the leather against the length of the neck.

The tail should be brushed in the direction of its natural curl from the base outward and on up to the tip from the curve outward. You will find that the tail in a direct line from the saddle will be covered with flat, smooth hair while the feathering grows from underneath. You will find this presents two "sides" of the tail to be brushed.

If your dog objects strenuously to medication, place the fingers over the dog's muzzle with the thumb on roof of the mouth, and put entire hand in his mouth. A dog cannot easily bite an entire fist but could bite two fingers. After the pill has been put down the throat, close the mouth and hold it for a few seconds until the dog has swallowed the pill. Rubbing the throat will sometimes hasten this. Always be sure the pill is down. Many dogs are clever at hiding pills in a back corner of their mouths until you aren't looking and then spit them out. You find them only when it's too late for another pill to do them any good.

The feet are usually the first part of the dog to get dirty. They should be brushed in a semi-circular direction along with the anatomy of the foot and from the leg outward. The hocks and elbows should receive special attention, since bones are prominent in these areas and the friction and wear on these spots makes the hair tend to tangle and mat.

At approximately one year of age you will find your Afghan Hound is about to get his saddle. This smooth strip of different-colored hair (except in all-black dogs) is another distinguishing feature characteristic of the breed. It is usually a few inches wide and runs from the base of the neck down the back and past the prominent hip bones to the end of the croup.

The hair may fall out completely and all at once, or it may be a slow process taking several months, with more and more of the soft puppy coat falling away with each brushing. It might be necessary to brush a little harder to get out the dead hairs completely, but usually the dog will clear in the normal course of brushing. Once in evidence, the saddle should be brushed with the lay of the hair—down the back from the neck toward the tail.

Your biggest problem in grooming, particularly until your dog has completely shed his puppy coat, will be mats. Little bits of debris that work their way into the coat, accompanied by bits of dead hair that doesn't get brushed away completely, will cause these tangles. If not taken care of promptly these tangles develop into mats. Mats have a way of getting even "mattier" and eventually will have to be cut out if allowed to go too far.

It is next to impossible to hide or cover up the unmistakable hole left in the coat when it has been necessary to cut out a mat. At its best, the amazing silky coat gives the glorious illusion of "floating" when the dog is in action, and this illusion is broken if the coat has become damaged or cut in any way.

Should you find a bad tangle or mat, brush away the surrounding hair and take the mat in your hand. Take a little bit at a time and shred it gently with your fingers, working it apart. When you comb and carefully and gently work it apart a little bit at a time, start at the end of the tangle and shred it up toward the body. When the hair is separated, start brushing gently also from the ends of the hair gradually up toward the body, until all the hair is free. When it is completely combed out, brush the hair back in with the rest of the coat.

112

You might also find it helps with a conscientious objector if you tuck
the leg under your arm as shown above. If he becomes extremely restless it sometimes helps to groom another part of the body, coming
back to the feet a little later.

There are various kinds of coat conditioners that can help you keep your dog well groomed. These are on sale at all pet shops. Which, if any, of these you use is largely a matter of preference. It should actually be a matter of which will best suit your dog's needs. Some of these preparations are strictly cleaning aids, and others help keep the coat free of "electricity," help retard tangles, etc., but one thing is certain. They all make the dog smell divine. Dogs with skin that is inclined to be dry or scaly should have dressings that contain more lanolin or other oils. These are applied with an atomizer and brushed into the coat.

If your Afghan Hound is exceptionally active in the fields or woods or is a city dog where soot and excessive street dirt plague him, you will more than likely want to use one of the dry shampoos or lather dry baths between actual tub baths. These also are for sale at all the pet shops. But do not expect miracles from these preparations. *You* must groom and feed properly to maintain the good health that will normally give your Afghan Hound the lustrous coat he is meant to have.

Cleaning your dogs ears is reasonably simple, though great caution should be used in this sensitive area. Cotton on an orange stick, or baby swab can be used. If you clean your dogs ears once a week or when necessary, any serious problems can usually be avoided.

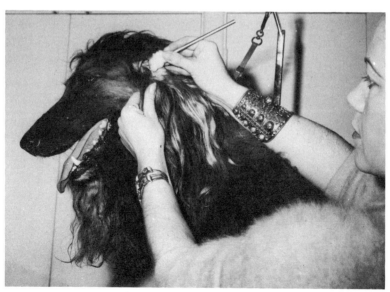

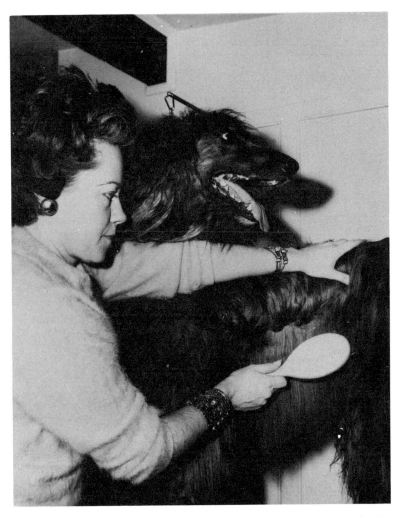

The Afghan's long silky coat should be brushed in layers in the direction in which the coat falls. Using the side of the arm, hold the coat up and use the brush to brush coat back to its natural position.

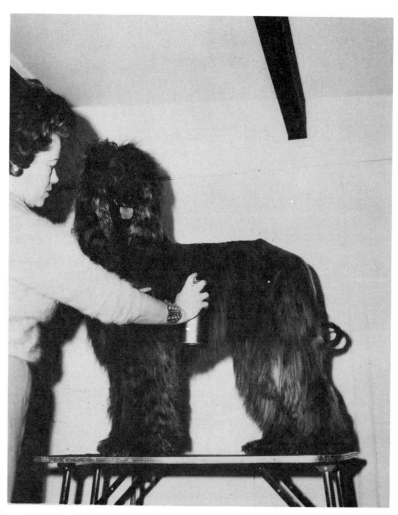

After you have groomed the dog's entire coat it is permissible to spray one of the popular grooming aids on him to help keep the hair in place and eliminate electricity. These grooming aids are available at your local petshop.

BATHING THE ADULT AFGHAN HOUND

There are probably as many theories on how, and how often, to bathe a dog as there are dog owners. There is, however, no set rule on frequency or method, although it is certain that show dogs, or dogs that are outdoors a great deal in all kinds of weather and still spend time indoors with the family, will require a bath now and then. With dogs the size of Afghan Hounds you'll make things easier for yourself if you use the bathtub. The drainage is ideal for the several rinsings that will be necessary, and a hand spray or length of hose can be attached to the faucet where there is adequate water pressure to speed the process.

The successful soaping that will clean your dog thoroughly can best be achieved if your dog is drenched well with warm water first. Start at the withers with the hose and work backwards. Save the head until very last. You will find your dog stays warmer and is less restless if he gets used to the feel of the water on his body before having the stream of water directed over his eyes.

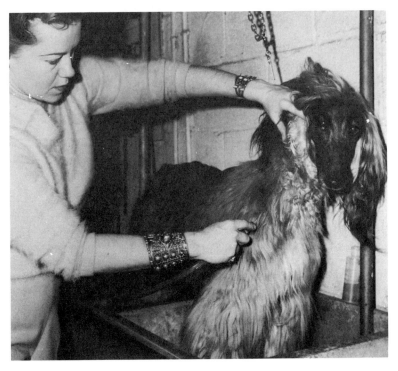

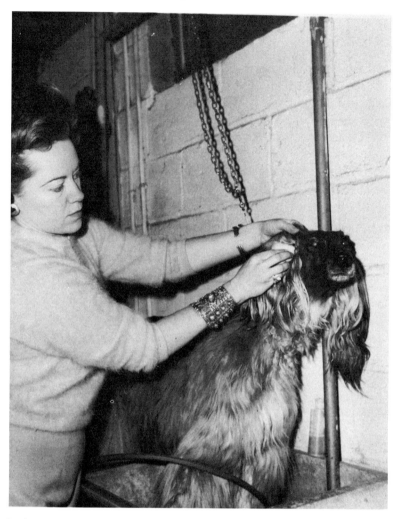

Bathing a dog is hard work at best, but if you don't know a few of the "tricks of the trade" with a large, long-haired dog it can be a disaster, ending up with everyone and everything equally wet and soapy. Basement washtubs can be a blessing for the partition in the middle prevents the dog from sitting down. Place back feet in one tub and front feet in the other. If you can suspend a leash or chain from the ceiling to attach to a collar it can help also. The next step is then to place cotton in the ears, as shown above. This not only keeps soap and water out during the wash, but helps keep down the noise of the dryer later on. Have your hose and shampoo ready and close at hand at this point and you're ready to begin.

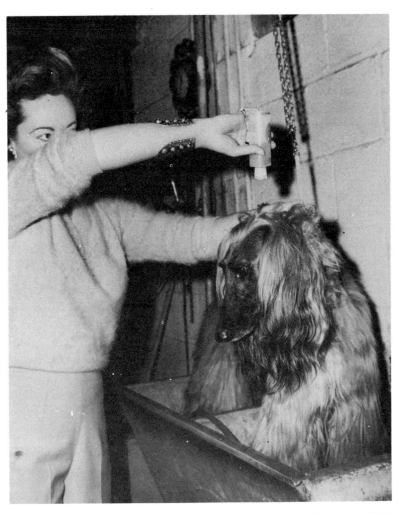

Once the coat is thoroughly drenched with water work up a thick lather with one of the better dog shampoos. Make sure the soap gets all the way to the skin, and be just as sure that after you've lathered him twice that you rinse all the shampoo out of the coat. Place the hose as close to the skin as possible and separate the coat as you move along.

Before placing the dog in the tub you might wish to put a few drops of mineral oil in his eyes to prevent burning from soap suds that might splash in; you also might place bits of cotton in the ears to prevent soapy water from entering them. Check your dog's footing. A ribbed rubber bath mat placed in the bottom of the tub will prevent him from slipping, and you'll find the dog will be much less troublesome and easier to handle when he's on firm footing.

Dog shampoos are preferable to cake soap, and two thorough soapings should be sufficient if the coat has been soaked to the skin with water before the first application of shampoo. Rinsings should continue until every last bit of shampoo is washed away. This cannot be stressed enough. Any soapy residue or shampoo that is left behind will make the hair gummy, dull, and lifeless, and will dry the skin as well.

You should check your dog's teeth, periodically, for tartar. You should also know how to show the bite to a judge if you intend to show your dog. Here again, place the fingers firmly over the muzzle and use thumb and forefinger to raise the skin and nose. With the other hand use your thumb to pull down lower lip. To show a judge the back teeth use all fingers to raise the entire top lip.

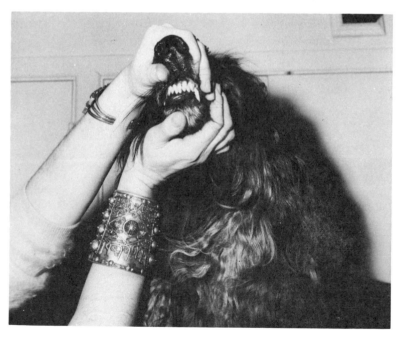

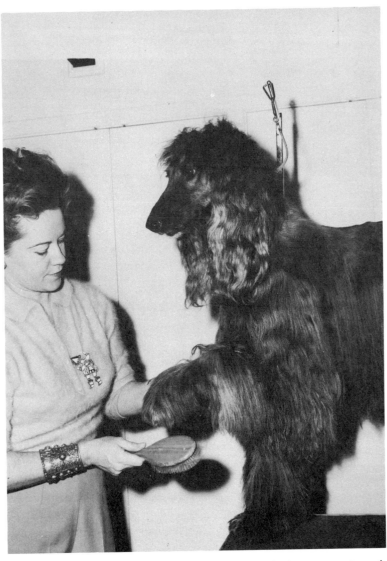

Dogs in general, and Afghan Hounds in particular, are extremely sensitive about their feet. Feet are essential to the dog's survival and he prefers not to have them tampered with by anyone. So be sure to be especially gentle in both your approach and your grooming. Hold the paw gently and brush in a semi-circle. If you find your dog gets restless, change back and forth from foot to foot and be even more gentle about it.

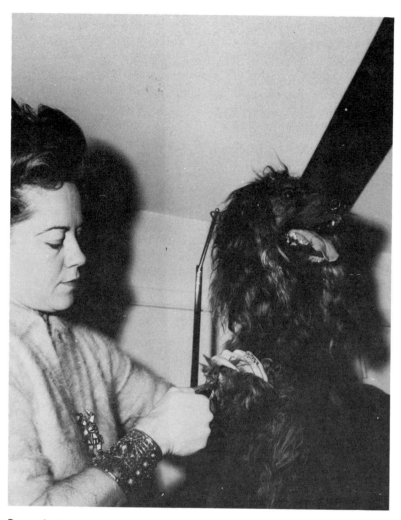

Dogs that are very active and run free usually manage to keep their claws at the proper length. Others require cutting now and again, especially if they are show dogs. There are proper claw clippers available at all petshops. Extreme care should be used not to cut the nail too far back. If you cut too far back you will find there is considerable bleeding. Hold the paw as shown above with the thumb pressing up between the toes to help spread them for easier cutting.

When rinsing it is best to use a wide spray. Start at the head, rinsing down the neck to the body, taking care to lift and separate the hair by layers, spreading with the fingers to allow the water to reach all the way to the skin. Don't just dump the water over the dog's head. Grab the muzzle firmly in one hand, tilt the head up and back, and pour the water down the head and neck from a point just behind the eyes.

After the head, body, and tail are done, the feet and legs should have additional and particular attention, since the rinsing water that remains in the bottom of the tub or doesn't run off quickly enough will cling to the feet. Rinse them once again until you are convinced the soap has gone completely. Then do it once again for good measure.

If you choose to use a hair rinse on your Afghan Hound it is now time to apply it. Some prefer creme rinses, others lemon or vinegar. Any of these will give the coat an extra sheen and luster. Another light water rinsing after this rinse is applied and you are almost ready to start the drying process. But let the dog drip-dry for a few minutes

Mrs. Louise French Schneider shown with Ch. Windtryst's Afire and Ch. Agha Kaimaakan of Arthea. A photograph of great beauty.

first. Not long enough to get a chill, of course, but long enough to prevent a water trail between the tub and grooming table. Then stand back. It's time for him to shake himself. If you can get a turkish towel over him before he does, so much the better for your walls!

THE DRYING PROCESS

While the dryer (or vacuum cleaner attachment) is warming up, take your towels and get rid of the excess water that will be dripping

When the dog has been rinsed clean, let him drip for a moment then squeeze dry with turkish towels. Stand him on a towel on the grooming table with another towel over him to prevent a chill.

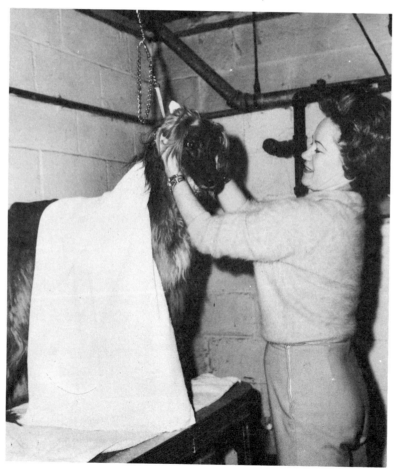

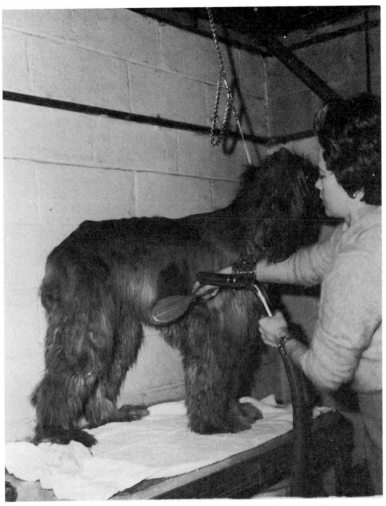

Using a clean brush, professional dog dryer, or the attachment on a vacuum cleaner, start to dry the dog. It is best not to brush too hard when the coat is still quite wet. Try to separate the hair until most of the surface moisture is gone, then begin grooming in layers. Dry the dog evenly all over, rather than in just one area at a time. When the dog is completely dry, be sure to remember to remove the cotton from his ears!

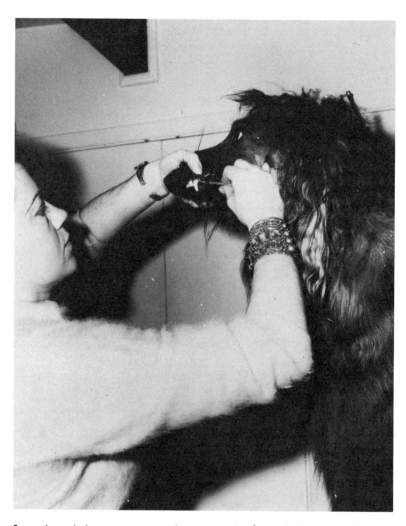

Sometimes it is necessary to clean your dog's teeth. Your veterinarian can do this, or if you are equipped with a "scaler," you can do it yourself. Start at the gum and scrape down the length of the tooth. For the lower jaw, start at the gum and scrape upwards. Scalers are usually available at petshops, or kennel suppliers, or perhaps your dentist will let you have one of his second hand scalers for your dog.

from the coat. Pressing the hair flat against the body and rubbing your hands down over the dog will take off a great deal of the excess. Try to avoid any circular motion with the towel. It is definitely conducive to tangling the hair and will pose a problem later on.

When the dryer has reached room temperature, start using the brush, working within the current of warm air. Allowing about a foot of space for you to work in between the blower and the dog, brush downward in layers, separating the hair down to the skin as

When brushing from the hock down, you will best be able to brush the full length of the hair if you place the dog's feet at the extreme edge of the table so that the hair can be brushed out, back, and down without hitting the table.

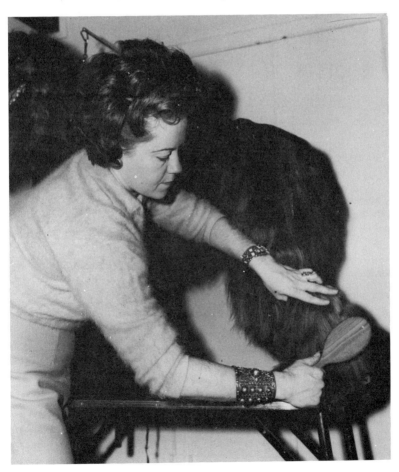

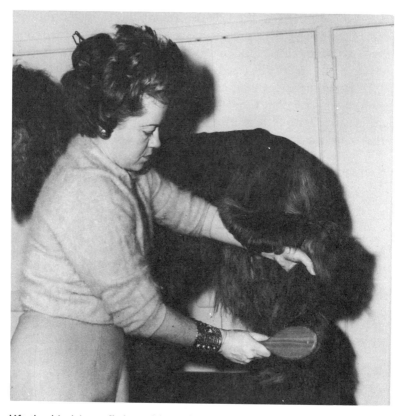

Lift the hind leg off the table to brush the front of the rear feet. Hair on the leg can be held away by the side of the arm. Here again the brushing is in a semi-circular direction around the toes.

you go. An Afghan Hound should never be left dry on the outside and wet next to the skin. So don't bathe your dog unless you are fully prepared to finish the job once you've started it. Allow for plenty of drying time. Move the dryer frequently all over the body, so that the dog dries evenly and not just in one spot. He'll brush out better if he's not too wet in one spot and too dry in another.

BATHING THE PUPPY

Here again there are two schools of thought on the advisability of bathing the very young puppy. If you are an advocate of the bath, the same technique can be used for the puppy that is advised for the grown dog. Keep them free of drafts and *never* leave a puppy only

The curved surface bristle brush should be used for the long hair on the tail. The tail should be held up and brushed in the direction of its natural curve.

One of the most wonderful characteristics of the Afghan Hound is his sleek and smooth saddle that runs from the base of the neck right down to the tail. It is advisable to use a softer brush with a flat bristle surface and stroke on this area. It should always be brushed in the direction in which it grows. Start at the base of the neck and continue down to the tail.

partially dry.

If you believe a bath endangers a puppy unnecessarily, it is wise to know about the dry shampoos mentioned earlier when a cleaning job seems advisable. These dry shampoos, plus regular brushings, will keep the puppy clean as well as stimulate the hair follicles and encourage the natural hair oils and growths of coat.

GROOMING BEHAVIOR

If your Afghan Hound wiggles and squirms and backs off and fights you every bit of the way when grooming time rolls around, chances are you're being a little too rough. True enough, there are dogs that just never get to like being groomed, and these dogs require extra patience and, quite possibly, extra work, since they will employ every scheme known to canines to put you off and hamper progress. But more than likely if you meet resistance it's because the dog is genuinely uncomfortable.

The main thing is to be gentle; be even more gentle in the sensitive areas such as the groin, the feet, under the tail, around the eyes, etc. The calmest of dogs will flinch when he sees the bristles of a brush or the shiny teeth of a steel comb flashing overhead. You can be pretty brisk on the body, the chest, saddle, etc., but such fervor in the tender regions can resemble Chinese torture.

Grooming your dog will probably never seem easy, but it can be a gratifying experience for both dog and master if approached with common sense and patience. Let your dog see that you take a definite pride in taking care of him. He will appreciate this interest and gentleness, and it will result in a closer communication between you and your dog through this personal relationship. And he'll certainly look a lot better for the correct care.

Chapter VII
Environment

FEEDING

Perhaps the most important of all aspects in the care and health of your Afghan Hound is diet. Meat, meal, milk, vitamins, egg yolks, dog biscuits, certain vegetables, wheat germ, etc., in the proper quantities help to make up a well-balanced diet that will keep your dog a happy, healthy specimen.

Since the capacity and size of the individual dog determines the amount of food he should consume each day, we'll not go into quantitative measures in regard to feeding. You can find quite accurate guides according to breed on the labels of most products you buy. In time you will learn your dog's capacity and can feed minimum or

Ch. Shahti Ben Kajar, at the age of ten, plays foster mother to a second litter of kittens. Shahti is owned by Mary Sheldon.

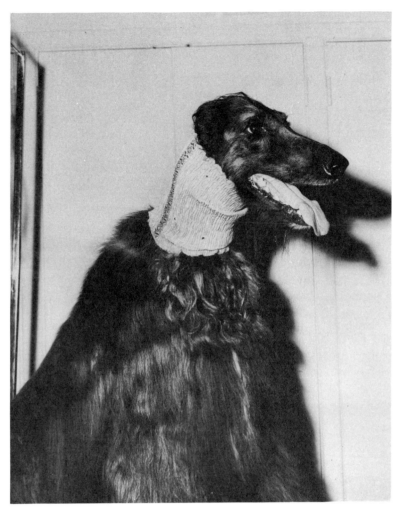

It is almost mandatory to keep your Afghan Hound's ears out of his food. This can be accomplished in many ways. The fancy snood or "hat" pictured above is one way, the top of a ladies' stocking is another, some even use pinch clothes pins. However, the most effective way so far seems to be to cut out the toe of a man's stretch sock. Then pull the cuff back over the head and push the ears into the heel on the back of the head.

maximum amounts according to the recommended diet. When you buy your new puppy the current and proper diet and approximate amounts of each ingredient should be given to you by the kennel owner or breeder.

Dog magazines and other publications devoted to dogs are often helpful on how and what to feed at various ages.

With the good health that stems from proper diet a dog will often overcome poor environment, can better withstand unfavorable climate and weather conditions, keep his resistance to disease at a peak, and in general can be a more alert, useful companion.

LIVING QUARTERS

In spite of all that's been said about the protective coat of the Afghan Hound, we must caution about the dangers of dampness and violent temperature changes when it comes to the health of your dog. The rugged outdoor Afghan Hound of yesterday could withstand the elements much better than the domesticated dogs of today, which live

A rather whimsical moment in the life of Canadian best in show winner, Int. Ch. Rudika of Blakeen. "Deeka," a daughter of Int. Ch. Rudiki of Pride's Hill, originally owned by Mrs. Sherman Hoyt and Marion Florsheim, was later sold to Mr. and Mrs. Charles Costabile, who furthered her fine show career.

A hardwood ramp is excellent for the dogs to come in and go out of their kennels by themselves. The ramp is good for strengthening hindquarters and legs. Crushed, three-quarter inch bluestone makes an excellent floor for a yard if it does not have a smooth concrete base. The bluestone dries quickly and is easy to keep clean. It is also good for an Afghan Hound's feet.

both indoors and outdoors. While the Afghan Hound still can withstand excessive heat or extreme cold, sudden change can be treacherous, particularly with puppies.

Dogs that are born and brought up outdoors quite naturally adjust to weather changes. But it is sheer folly for a dog to sleep indoors by a furnace or stove or hock-deep in a comforter on his master's bed one night and to spend the next night outdoors in an unheated barn or bare-floored doghouse or garage. A dog can stand the cold while he's running around outside, but he should have a dry bed protected from wind and rain in winter and a cool, shady place to sleep in summer.

The matter of what to use for a dog's bed is optional. Some dog owners prefer hay, or cedar shavings for outdoors, and blanketing or newspaper liners indoors. It is also a matter of preference on whether the bed itself should be metal or wood. Chances are your Afghan Hound will choose his own bed. They like to sleep high up where they can keep an eye on things, preferring even a table at times to the coziest of beds. Many breeders buy army cots for their Afghan Hounds . . . and if placed beneath a window where he can look outside, you'll find he's a most happy fella.

Chapter VIII
Showing your Afghan Hound

Let us assume that after a few weeks or a few months of tender loving care, you feel your Afghan Hound puppy is developing nicely and perhaps even exceeds your wildest expectations of being a show quality puppy. Of course, every Afghan Hound owner is prejudiced.

Ch. Holly Hill Desert Wind, owned by Mrs. Cheever Porter, six times a best in show winner and 30 hound group firsts on his show record to date. "Windy" was second ranking Afghan Hound for 1963 and 7th ranking dog in the hound group ratings. He was bred by Sue A. Kauffman. Photo by William Brown.

You can't own an Afghan Hound without loving it and admiring it beyond comparison. But if you are sincerely interested in showing and making a champion of your dog you must realize that it is very possible for a dog to have one, and very possibly more, faults. The best way to appraise an Afghan Hound's worth and degree of perfection is to put him before an accredited judge, or judges, in a show ring.

SHOW PROCEDURES

It is not possible to show a puppy for points toward a championship until it reaches the age of six months. When your dog reaches this eligible age, your local kennel club can and will send you, in response to your request, a premium list containing names and addresses of local dog superintendents who are holding dog shows in your area in the near future. Send for these premium lists, which will contain entry blanks as well as all pertinent information regarding the show.

Best In Show winner in Romford, England, British and American Ch. Bletchingley Ragman of Scheherezade, rests on his laurels after winning this coveted title.

Ch. Crown Crest Khalifah, in a classic headstudy taken at the Afghan Hound Club of America Specialty Show. She is owned by Sahadi Kennels.

To be eligible for point-show competition in an American Kennel Club approved show a dog must fit within other specific qualifications in addition to the six-months-old age requirement. He must be purebred, which means he and his sire and dam are registered with the A.K.C. And there must be no alterations or falsifications regarding sex or appearance. Females must not be altered, males must have two testicles, and no dyes or powders or colorings can be used to change or enhance or distract from the natural appearance of the dog. Any lameness or deformity or major deviation from the standard for the breed constitutes a disqualification.

With this in mind, groom your dog accordingly, and to the best of your knowledge and ability in the areas provided for grooming at the shows you can walk into the show ring with great pride of

Ch. Crown Crest Sancy and Ch. Crown Crest Vegas Ghambler of Belden, best Afghan Hound brace at the International Kennel Club shown here with owner Leo Goodman and judge J. H. Aldrich. These two striking black-masked silvers were the foundation stock of Mr. Goodman's Belden Kennels. Photo by William Brown.

Ch. Akaba's Top Brass, owned, bred, and shown by Lois Boardman. "Brassy" was the winner of the hound group at the Westminster Kennel Club in 1962. He went on to win the title of top-winning Afghan Hound in the United States for that year.

ownership. The judge will rule according to the American Kennel Club approved set of standards for the breed and will allow each dog a certain amount of time and consideration. It is never permissible to consult the judge regarding either your dog or his decision while you are still in the ring. An exhibitor never speaks unless spoken to, and then only to answer such questions as the judge may ask: the age of the dog, for instance, or when asking you to show the dog's bite.

You will be asked to gait your dog around the ring with the others in his class, to gait him individually in a T formation for the judge's individual attention, and to set the dog up in a show stance for individual examination. To learn the correct show stance, it is wise

Teaching your dog to gait along with you is best accomplished by using a short leash to make certain his head stays in a line with your body. Gentle tugs in either direction, or up if he tries to drag behind, or sniff the ground, is usually all that are necessary to get the idea across.

to study the position of the Afghan Hounds shown in many of the photographs accompanying this book. That is to say, the front legs should be straight down from the shoulders, well under the body, with the hind legs pulled slightly back to show hind quarter angulation, head high, tail curled, and top line level. Wins will be awarded on the basis of the degree of the dog's qualifications, and there are first through fourth place ribbons awarded in each of the five classes. Unless stated otherwise in the premium list sent to you by the show superintendent, the five regular classes to be entered at an all-breed show are as follows:

PUPPY CLASS—For dogs between six months and one year of age.

NOVICE—For dogs which have never won a first prize ribbon except in the puppy class.

Ch. Sahadi Comanche Brave Eagle finishing for his championship at the Bucks County Kennel Club under judge R. Beale. "Ego" is owned by Ellen Steinschneider O'Leske, and is a son of Ch. Crown Crest Jesi Jhaimz, out of Ch. Crown Crest Khalifah. Photo by William Brown.

BRED BY EXHIBITOR—This class is for dogs you have bred yourself and can only be shown by you or a member of your immediate family. No champions are eligible for this class.

AMERICAN BRED—For dogs (and here again champions of record are not eligible) bred and born in this country.

OPEN—This class is for all dogs. You may even enter a champion. However, it is specifically for dogs that are full grown and are aiming for points toward championship status, though points may be awarded to the winners of any one of the five classes.

Ribbons are awarded and the colors are as follows: first, blue; second, red; third, yellow; fourth, white. Once the winners of each class are determined, first place dogs enter the ring again, and the best

Group first from the classes over champion competition at the Willimantic Kennel Club Show, Sahadi Apache Geronimo and owner-handler Joan Brearley, pose with judge Anna Katherine Nicholas. Geronimo is a son of Ch. Crown Crest Jesi Jhaimz out of Ch. Crown Crest Khalifah. Photo by Evelyn Shafer.

The desired Afghan Hound silhouette is best shown in this pose, which a dog show judge expects to see. The head should be high, legs straight down from the shoulders, and hind legs pulled slightly back to show hindquarter angulation.

from one of the five classes is awarded the title of Winners Dog and is given the points toward championship.

The same classes are then held for the bitches. Points are awarded to the Winners Dog and Winners Bitch in accordance with a scale of points established by the American Kennel Club, and the number of points you would win each time out is based on the number of dogs competing in these classes. This scale of points varies in different sections of the country, but the schedule is published in the front of each dog show catalogue. These points may differ even between the dogs and the bitches at the same show, but you may win additional points by winning Best of Winners, if there are fewer dogs entered than bitches, or vice versa. Points never exceed five at any one show.

Ch. Monarc's Nubia, owned by Gloria Britain. This lovely bitch, pictured here going Best of Breed over specials at just 13 months of age, now has several group placings among her show winnings, and was Best of Opposite Sex at the parent club Specialty Show in 1964. Photo by William Brown.

Ch. Sashay el Sayyad, bred, owned and shown by Grace Beyer. Daughter of Ch. Crown Crest Kabul, Sashay is shown here taking winners bitch under judge Kay Finch. Photo by Roberts.

A total of fifteen points must be won to constitute a championship; these points must be won under at least three different judges. Anything from a three- to a five-point win is considered a *major* award, and one- and two-point shows are minor wins. A dog must earn at least two majors, under two different judges, to achieve championship status, in addition to the balance of points.

Once the Winners Dog is determined, when the judge has had the opportunity to examine the best of each of the five class winners, plus a Reserve Winner which is his second choice dog from the classes, he proceeds to the bitch classes. When the Winners Bitch and Reserve Winners Bitch have been selected, the Winners Dog and the Winners Bitch return to the ring to compete against one another for the Best of Winners title. The dog or bitch to win Best of Winners is then eligible to enter the Specials class, a class set aside for dogs and bitches which have already achieved their championships, and may compete with these champions for the coveted Best of Breed title.

Should the Best of Breed title go to a male, a female is then chosen for the Best of Opposite Sex title. If a female is chosen, a male takes Best of Opposite Sex. If you are entered at a Specialty Show (a show where only one breed is shown), and you take the Best of Breed award, you have attained the pinnacle of success, for it also means a Best In Show win. At a Specialty Show, if you are entered in the classes, you might win Best Puppy in Show, or Best American Bred in Show, or Best Bred by Exhibitor in show. Best of Breed wins at all-breed shows mean you are eligible to move on to the Hound Group judging.

When exhibiting Afghan Hounds, quite naturally you would be in the Hound Group, where first through fourth place ribbons are

Int. Ch. Rana of Chaman of Royal Irish. His show record at the time of his retirement was three best in show awards, seventeen times best hound, forty-two group placings, and forty-eight bests of breed.

Khabira Zahrin, owned by Werner and Mary Sheldon, winner of the adult dog Hound Group at a Staten Island Kennel Club match show.

awarded to those dogs or bitches which place first through fourth of all the hound breeds at the show. The other five groups are the Sporting, Working, Terrier, Toy, and Non-Sporting. The first place winners in each of these six groups again enter the ring where a judge determines his choice for a dog which is declared Best In Show.

MATCH SHOWS

While it is not possible to show a puppy for points toward a championship until the age of six months, many parent breed clubs as well as all-breed clubs frequently stage annual or semi-annual Match Shows, where it is possible for beginners to show their dogs for prizes and ribbons in a "mock" dog show. Here, where all rules are adhered to without the points being given, the age limit is reduced and a class is provided for three- to six-month-old puppies, and six- to nine-month-old puppies, as well as nine- to twelve-month-old puppies.

For those seriously interested in showing their Afghan Hounds to a championship in the future, these match shows provide important experience for both dog and owner. Class categories may vary slightly from point shows, but basically they go through all the motions of a regular point show. Here again, the best way to find out about these shows is to contact the parent club and your local all-breed club. Names and addresses of club corresponding secretaries can usually be secured through the dog column in the town newspaper.

There is a nominal entry fee for a Match Show, usually in the

Ch. Zaadulla of Arthea and Winonie of Ghazni owned by Doris Wheeler. Winonie is a litter sister to the very famous Ch. Taejon of Crown Crest, and was foundation bitch for Mrs. Wheeler's Kandulla Kennels.

Marion Florsheim awards best of breed to Ch. Crown Crest Kabul at the Afghan Hound Club of California. He is owned by Mary Stephenson. John Buchanan handled "Kabbie" to his victory over an entry of seventy-four Afghan Hounds including thirteen other champions. Photo by Joan Ludwig.

amount of a dollar per entry; unlike those of the point shows, these entries can be made the day of the show right on the show grounds. They are also unbenched and provide a very relaxed, congenial atmosphere for the amateur, which helps to make the ordeal of one's first adventures in the show ring less nerve-racking.

WHAT A JUDGE LOOKS FOR IN THE SHOW RING

One of the most frequent questions asked a breeder when he sells a show dog to a new customer is: what does the judge look for when he judges a dog in the show ring? This question is easy for me to answer, since I have been judging dogs myself for many years.

I could go on at great length pointing out the most obvious as well as the finer points a judge looks for when giving a comparative appraisal of dogs in a ring at a dog show. But perhaps the most concise and descriptive guide to the most important points was published in the September, 1963 issue of the *Northern California Afghan Hound Club News* bulletin, when I was invited to write such an analysis of how I judge a dog. This is what I wrote:

"From a judge's point of view, my first impression must be that the dog entering the ring possesses the dignity, aloofness, and expression that suggests it is every inch an Afghan Hound. In personal examination of the dog my first concern is the bone structure. If the skeleton of the dog is sound, the dog will possess the second most important thing I look for—proper movement. I look for the Afghan

Ch. Tajmir's Redstone Rocket, co-owned by breeder Patricia Sinden and Joan Fantl. Rocket was the winner of the Afghan Hound Club of America Specialty Show in 1964. Rocket also has 27 Hound Group firsts and 55 Best of Breeds to his credit. Tauskey Photo

Ch. Sahadi Sessu, with owner-handler Nancy McCarthy Gardner, winning best of breed at the Kennel Club of Northern New Jersey under judge Leo Murphy. Young sire of four champions to date in one litter, Sessu is sired by Int. Ch. Shirkhan of Grandeur out of Ch. Crown Crest Khalifah. Breeder Joan Brearley. Photo by William Brown.

Hound that moves soundly, reaches out with those big front feet, and pushes hard with a strong rear. I do not like Afghan Hounds that prance like circus horses. Thirdly, I look for strength in the hindquarters and good heads. Heavily-headed Afghan Hounds and those with wobbly hind ends are becoming far too prevalent in the breed today. Next I look for good disposition and showmanship. Too many dogs show badly, and this is the fault of the owner. Many good dogs go down to inferior specimens because they do not make the most of themselves in the show ring. Also the snappy specimens or "cry babies" that won't show, ruin their wins when this is also the fault of their owner. A good showman and an even-tempered dog is as much a part of exhibiting a dog as making sure every hair is in place. After showmanship and disposition I take into consideration coat and

153

coat pattern, and then start narrowing down to individual, but equally important, points.

I feel I must clarify further, in this almost itemized list, the first of the points I look for in the Afghan Hound—that of bone structure. With the proper bone structure your dog will possess the length of head and neck we so desire, the well laid back shoulder, the strong, straight top-line, the length of tail, the depth of brisket and straight front, and the hind angulation so essential to our coursing hounds. Everything good about the Afghan Hound "hangs on" to that skeleton. It is one of the sheerest delights to me as a judge to "get my hands on" that skeleton and check it out for perfection. It's a wonderful experience to discover what is really under all that beautiful coat. And as a judge I have made it a firm policy never to pass judgment on any Afghan Hound until I have had this pleasure!"

AFGHAN HOUNDS IN OBEDIENCE

The first Companion Dog (abbreviated C.D. or CD) title was awarded to an Afghan Hound by the American Kennel Club in 1939 and was announced officially in the October issue of the *American Kennel Gazette, Pure-Bred Dogs* magazine. The name of the dog to win this distinction for the Afghan Hound breed was Doreborn's Kamu, owned by C. Ross Hamilton, Jr. Kamu went on to earn a Companion Dog Excellent title as well. Companion Dog Excellent (abbreviated C.D.X. or CDX) is one step above the Companion Dog title.

Mr. Hamilton, Kamu's owner, is today a prominent conformation judge as well as obedience judge; he officiated in the Afghan Hound ring at the Westminster Kennel Club Show in February of 1957, at which time he gave the Best of Breed award to Ch. Shirkhan of Grandeur, which went on to win Best In Show.

As of the present day there are just a few Afghan Hounds which have won the title of Utility Dog (abbreviated U.D. or UD). The first was Gini Withington's Koh-I-Baba. Several of the Withington dogs hold obedience titles. Virginia Mika is another breeder-exhibitor who has been active in the obedience rings. Both women, with their beautiful hounds, have done much to prove the ability of the Afghan Hound in obedience.

We must recall that for a long time it was believed that the Afghan Hound did not lend itself to obedience training. This may or may

An Afghan Hound in action. The great Ch. Koh-I-Baba, U.D. Koh-I-Baba was the first American U.D. in the breed. Photo by Joan Ludwig.

Show ring manners are important. While the judge is going over your dog, you are expected to stand away so that he may examine him without hindrance. The best way to teach your dog the stand for examination is illustrated above. Set your dog up, then step directly in front of him and command "stay."

not have been true, depending perhaps on the particular dog and its teacher. It is known that many Afghan Hounds are not given to taking orders, or "snapping to" on command. They are far too independent by nature. However, the A.K.C. records now prove this to be untrue. By nature, the Afghan Hound is a slower-moving animal (except when hunting) and should not necessarily be expected to carry out commands with the speed of some of the other breeds.

All things considered, the totals of awarded titles, taking into account the comparative scarcity of Afghan Hounds in this country until the past few decades, are quite impressive. They should dispel any fears or doubts for the Afghanite who wishes to enter the obedience field with his Afghan Hound. In recent years many Afghan Hounds have been observed going from the breed ring over to the obedience ring, or to Junior Showmanship competition, at the dog shows. Perhaps the most outstanding demonstration of this is the record acquired by Miss Patricia Leary (later, Mrs. Erik Thomee, wife of the professional handler) of Pluckemin, New Jersey. She

Su-Ric's Safar, C.D., C.D.X., owned by Robert Luzietti, is one of a very few Companion Dog Excellent Afghan Hounds in the country. This informal photograph shows her in front of owner's home.

Teaching your dog to lie down can be difficult with this large breed.
If he doesn't get the idea with the lowered hand motion and the
command "down," it can often be accomplished by placing the leash
under your foot and pulling up on your end of it, and repeating the
command, "down!"

158

Ivardon Tufan Khan, U.D. Tufan won his Utility Dog title in July of 1953 — one of the few U.D. Afghan Hounds ever to accomplish this feat. Bred by Dr. William Ivens, he is co-owned by Ruth Thompson, his trainer.

piloted her black and tan bitch, Ch. Lala Rookh of Estioc, from a Best In Show award at the Afghan Hound Club of America's Specialty Show in 1956 to top Junior Showmanship honors at Westminster two days later at Madison Square Garden.

A more recent example of course is the remarkable record established in Junior Showmanship by Miss Jennifer Sheldon. Twice to date she has handled her Afghan Hound, Ch. Khabiri of Grandeur, to Best In Show wins and won the Stewards Club of America Award for Champion Junior Handler of the Year in 1962. She has also placed second in Junior Showmanship at Westminster in 1962, 1963, and 1964.

Being dogs of exquisite and unusual appearance, Afghan Hounds of the past and present have distinguished themselves in many ways. Marion Foster Florsheim's Ch. Rana of Chaman of Royal Irish was active during World War II in raising funds for war relief organizations by making personal appearances. Rana, in appropriate costume, hosted a show—along with other canine friends, called "Calling All Dogs" at New York City's Ritz Towers Hotel in March, 1941. Rana was also in some Warner Brothers movies, as were the two Afghan Hounds imported by Zeppo Marx mentioned elsewhere in this book. In an article in an early issue of the *Afghan Bulletin*, authored by Marion Foster Florsheim, Lt. James T. Sharkey, U.S.C.G., tells of obedience training his Afghan Hound, Zombie of Dunrobbin, which served as mascot of his Coast Guard post. And from the early days up to the present day, more and more Afghan Hounds are being seen in advertisements and fashion features in newspapers and magazines, and they have also appeared in stage shows and on television.

HOW TO BEGIN OBEDIENCE TRAINING

There are several books available on obedience training. For those interested in attending classes at reputable schools, it is wise to contact the local dog club in your area for starting dates of their classes and requirements for entry, as well as cost. Classes usually meet once a week for one hour, and while you can train your dog yourself with the aid of a book, the experience the dog gains from actually participating with other dogs is very valuable. Practice time between classes is fifteen minutes once or twice daily. Needless to say, the "reward" system, never punishment or unnecessary roughness, is used in obedience training. If cruelty is used, the dog's spirit is broken and he will be no good to you as a pet or companion. The properly trained dog is a well-behaved member of the family and a joy to travel and visit with, and he will delight in pleasing you with his perfectly executed commands and general good behavior.

Chapter IX
Afghan Hound Racing

The most exciting thing to happen in the Afghan Hound fancy in the United States since the days of their first importation is the sport of racing—which is literally sweeping the country.

Since the first Shikari watched his pack of hunting Afghan Hounds race across the desert or scale the rocky tors of Afghanistan tracking prey, the striking beauty of the dog "in flight" has kindled a desire to see this great coursing hound in action. The fact that entirely too many of today's Afghan Hounds are content to sit in metropolitan apartments merely adorning brocade couches is leading many people to believe that this is now their sole purpose in life. But to those who

Rhyng Tayl Lynx, C.D., owned by Jonna Frosch, shown running in a park near her home. This-four-year old bitch holds three speed records for Afghan Hound racing in the Midwest. She has run 110 yards in 8 seconds on an oval track, 10 seconds for 200 yards on a straight track, and 18.8 seconds on a 272 yard horseshoe track.

Bucky, Tina and Chris round the bend in a practice heat during training at the Devi Baba Kennels.

truly enjoy these dogs as sporting companions there is forever the lingering desire to see them at their best: in pursuit of game or the lure.

And so it was that even the first people to import these dogs to England back in the early 1900's used them to hunt and to race. Mrs. Molly Sharpe of Dumfries, Scotland, had a team of racing Afghan Hounds back before World War I. Her Garrymhor Faiz-Bu-Hassid was one of her best and fastest racers of his day.

No accurate records were kept of the various distances and timings, however. We have only word-of-mouth accounts of Afghanites getting together on private estates and racing their hounds for sheer love of watching them on the run. The same thing was true in this country.

Understandably, Afghan Hound racing was discouraged in the United States lest it interfere with Greyhound racing, which has been big business for a long time. But in the early 1950's Bill and Gini Withington of California stimulated a great deal of interest by holding the first heats at their home in Pasadena. Now, almost fifteen years later, Bill and Gini are often called upon for help and advice in getting racing started in other sections of the country.

In January, 1960 interest in Afghan Hound racing came to fruition in another part of California when fourteen enthusiasts decided to get together in a Los Angeles suburb. A total of twenty-one dogs showed up for this initial endeavor, as well as myriads of curious passersby who were even less sure of what these proud owners and their shaggy dogs were trying to accomplish.

To say this first effort was chaotic is putting it mildly. Some dogs took off for the trees, some for the other dogs, some for home, and some for parts unknown. Fortunately, a few others did chase the lure. In spite of this inauspicious beginning, the thrill of the race inspired the crowd, and Afghan Hound racing became an established sport in Southern California.

Much has been learned and improved upon since these early beginnings. General club rules and regulations have been put into effect to establish the basis for more permanent ones, namely, national racing and coursing rules for Afghan Hounds, later on.

The most satisfactory tracks are four hundred feet or longer. More speed can be attained on a straight track than on the conventional oval or oblong. Muzzles, of course, are a must, since the most even-tempered dogs have been known to lose their heads in the excitement of completing a race. Owners prefer to prevent the scuffles that might ensue and ruin these valuable dogs.

Starting boxes are safest for a fair start. Thus no leash-held dog is given a head start by an over-zealous owner. Some of the racing clubs have applied a cooperative effort in building these starting boxes and supply them for the entrants. Other members prefer to build their own, as well as make their own muzzles out of soft leather.

A fur lure is the surest way to keep your race keen, though it need not necessarily be a scented one. Afghan Hounds, we must remember, are primarily sight hounds, and it's the movement of an object more than the scent of an object that piques their interest.

No definite conclusions have been reached as to speed in relation to the sex of the animal. There are as many—if not more—bitches which lead the pack as there are dogs. Nor does the size of the individual dog make an appreciable difference. Sheer love of the race seems to motivate the swiftness of foot, and only the most spirited and the best-conditioned of them can maintain their speed as the heats continue during a racing event.

IGNITION — Mounted on this car he can go in either direction and can do a lap in 5 seconds flat. He also operates the starting bell and starting box doors.

Fast break on a clear track during a racing session. Photo by Ben Burwell.

An alert dog will do well in the first heat, but it takes a dog in top condition, which has had roadwork in his training curriculum, to consistently maintain speed as the races continue. The number of heats is determined by the number of entries, and the winners of each heat then compete against each other until the top winner is determined. Four to six dogs racing at one time seems to be about the most comfortable limit for these events.

The speed these dogs attain in a race quite naturally varies. Each individual proud owner of a consistent winner can reel off individual timings reached by his dog on various occasions, since owners are most always found at track-side with a stopwatch in their hands. But club averages vary, because track lengths vary from club to club.

Dick and Georgiana Guthrie, who are largely responsible for the 1960 formation of the Afghan Coursing Associates Club, in California, claim that an avid racer in pursuit of a lure can attain twenty-nine miles an hour. On a 450-foot track an Afghan Hound can do the distance in 10.5 seconds. The less keen dog, which merely enjoys "running with the pack," averages only about twenty-three miles per hour, or 450 feet in 13.3 seconds.

These San Fernando Valley racing fans now run their hounds on a 600-foot track, fifteen feet wide. Their lure is towed by a hand-powered winch geared down to a thirty-five to one ratio, and mounted on a surveyor's tripod. The winding spool has a diameter of eight to ten inches. Their starting boxes, made by club members, have proven satisfactory at a width of nine inches, a height of thirty inches, and a length of thirty-six inches. They sometimes place low jumps along the track for added interest.

When racing was first begun in earnest, most clubs used the regular Greyhound racing rules. Time and experience proved certain modifications had to be made to suit our particular breed and some of the facilities available for those wanting to race. Now most clubs have their own rules or use those sent out by the clubs sponsoring

The racing line-up at the Devi Baba Kennels. Bucky, Christy, Bobbi, Mojud, Davy and Tina watch the track being put in readiness for the first race of the day. The clubhouse can be seen above the living quarters of these exquisite racing and show Afghan Hounds.

Christy at fourteen months of age. An experienced track dog with a stride that is his trainer's dream. Owned and raced by the Devi Baba Kennels, Christy poses during a grooming session in the tack room to prove an Afghan Hound can race and be beautiful.

racing events at the all-breed kennel club shows. An example of such a listing of rules that very probably would accompany the entry form follows:

RACING RULES FOR AFGHAN RACING EXHIBITIONS

1. All dogs must wear muzzles and collars while racing.
2. All dogs must be on lead except when racing.
3. No dogs or handlers shall be allowed on the track except those participating in the race then being conducted.
4. It is the responsibility of the owner or handler to retrieve his dog at the finish of a race, or at any time the dog stops running.
5. A bitch in season shall not be allowed to race or be anywhere on or near the track.
6. The Stewards have sole discretion to determine which dogs will run in any race, and to remove any dog from any race for misbehavior.

Ryng Tayl Lynx shown winning the run-off at the Kalamazoo dog show, where she went on to her speed record of 110 yards in 8 seconds. On another occasion Lynx raced against Whippets at Milwaukee and held the track record for five days, five races per day for each dog. She has her C.D. title, and is now working in obedience toward a C.D.X. title.

7. No dog will be allowed in any race unless a release form has been properly signed.
8. No person shall be allowed on the track at any time without permission of the Stewards.
9. All Afghan Hounds must be AKC registered or eligible to be registered.
10. Entry fee must accompany racing entry. Dogs need not be entered in conformation to be eligible for racing.
11. Choke collars are acceptable as racing equipment, and entrants must furnish their own collars.

Racing is now an established event at many of the all-breed dog shows around the country. Pioneer in this regard was the Chicago International show. Each year it continues to feature racing as a part of the regular show. Warren Fenn of Ohio was a witness to this event and took it upon himself to see that racing was established in his home state shortly thereafter. In August of 1962 the Ravenna, Ohio, kennel club began to feature Afghan Hound racing; it still does. The Santa Barbara, California, kennel club show, one of the top ten dog shows in the country, has featured racing since 1960.

Many other kennel clubs are planning to follow suit, but others are still reluctant, since some of these races bring out "unreliable entrants" which tend to confuse matters and lose the interest of the ringsiders. Local racing clubs must be made responsible for adequate training sessions prior to entries of their members at these all-breed events so that we put our best foot forward in bringing Afghan Hound racing to the highest level as an exciting sport.

In behalf of this endeavor the Northern California Afghan Hound Club contemplates scheduling a course in racing for their club members in the near future. They are also at work drawing up a set of racing rules for American Kennel Club approval for sight-hound coursing that might well be adopted by racing clubs all over the country.

The "home" track at the Devi Baba Kennels. As professionally equipped as any major track could be, this home race course is complete with night lights and an electrical squirrel lure named "Ignition." Guests of owners Pat and Gertrude Curnyn are invited to race their Afghan Hounds in guest colors. A movie was made for network television on the racing events at the Curnyns,' who are responsible for much of the favorable publicity given to the exciting sport of racing.

Another club, in another part of the country, has taken up still another form of Afghan Hound coursing. In February 1963 the New Mexico Dog Racing and Coursing Club decided, by vote of its stockholders, to devote two full days of their meet to Afghan Hound coursing exclusively. Member Pearson Crosby, of Albuquerque, reports that an entry fee of $10 was charged, two-thirds of which went into purses for winners, and one-third to cover club expenses. Entries were divided into two classes: over fourteen months old, and under fourteen months old. Name, age, sex, color, and marking information must be included on entry blanks along with the usual pertinent information required at such sporting events.

A field 1,000 feet long and 350 feet in width, with escape hatches for the live jackrabbits at the far end, is used, with Afghan Hounds coursing in pairs determined by previous drawings. The use of live rabbits, which has caused some adverse comments on occasion, does not necessarily mean random slaughter of live animals. Their escape hatches are numerous, and there are very few dogs as fast as jack-

Ch. Crown Crest Babaloo, one of the fastest Afghan Hound racing bitches in the country takes off after the lure at her private track. She is another of the foundation bitches at the Curnyn's Devi Baba Kennels.

"Bucky" posed and ready to go in his leather muzzle and silks, at his home track.

rabbits, yet a winner can be named by the time the rabbit has managed to escape the course.

With this type of coursing and the practice racing that must precede actual heats, the element of danger to the beautiful silky coats we must maintain on our show dogs is present. Many Afghanites have called even further attention to our breed by conducting this practice racing and schooling by putting the dogs in "long johns." Red underwear on an Afghan Hound viewed by unsuspecting observers from across a field can be a startling sight, but it does protect the coat from twigs, burs, leaves and such and still gives the dogs enough freedom to run and helps accustom them to wearing their racing blankets with their numbers on them.

In August, 1961 the Sunday newspaper supplement *This Week*

published a color cover story featuring Bill and Gini Withington's Afghan Hounds cavorting about the California countryside in their long red underwear. These dogs and other dogs thus attired never fail to arouse controversial comment wherever they appear.

Perhaps some day many of us, caught up in the surge of enthusiasm for racing, will be as fortunate as Pat and Gertrude Curnyn, a brother and sister team of Hanson, Massachusetts. Amid a woodland setting is a complete race track in their own backyard. A special tractor smooths the track between heats to make for a fast course, and a squirrel lure, appropriately named "Ignition," makes his countless rounds to keep the Curnyns' Devi Baba Afghan Hounds in perfect racing condition. On certain days the Curnyns invite visiting racing fans and their dogs to race in "guest colors."

"Bucky," a racing Afghan Hound owned by Gertrude Curnyn, models the wire schooling muzzle.

The wardrobe rack in the tack room at the Devi Baba Kennels. All the
silks match the starting box doors. Visitors' silks are seen in the foreground. They are made of the famous "Miller Jockey Colors" used on
every race track in the world.

All is in readiness for nighttime racing at the Devi-Baba Kennels
private race track.

Designed and supervised by Pat Curnyn, this private track has been photographed on many occasions, for many publications, and will be the subject of a television program. The publicity they have gotten for the breed will do much to make racing an even more popular sport in time to come. We can all look forward to the day when we might have our own race track, or be invited to the pleasure and such a marvelous track as the Curnyns maintain.

But in the meantime, as Afghan Hound racing fans, we now know that Afghan Hound racing is here to stay. Enthusiasm is increasing and clubs are continuing to sprout all over the country. It's encouraging to see that more and more all-breed kennel clubs are sponsoring racing events. The club members help to support racing by donating impressive trophies and helping, through newspapers and magazines, to publicize these events whenever possible. They encourage newcomers to race under their own colors and to spread the word about this sport to those who buy puppies from them. It is yet only a hope, but more and more talk is heard about a National Racing and Coursing Club exclusively for our Afghan Hounds, which have been known on many occasions to surpass the speed of Whippets and Greyhounds when they race together. It is becoming closer to reality with every passing day. It is no longer just a dream.

Chapter X
The Afghan Hound Club of America, Inc.

ORGANIZATION OF THE CLUB

In 1935 the parent Afghan Hound Club was formed in the United States with Q. A. Shaw McKean as its first president. But not until 1938 was it recognized by the American Kennel Club. In spite of a

Top winners of the 1963 Afghan Hound Club of America Specialty, Ch. Crown Crest Khalifah Best Opposite Sex and her son, Ch. Sahadi Shikari Best of Breed. Club president Donald A. Smith presents trophy with judge Kay Finch. Photo by Evelyn Shafer.

limited membership—only five attended that first meeting in 1935—the club members worked diligently to increase their membership and establish a headquarters for a breed club, and eventually to stage the first of the Afghan Hound Specialty Shows.

The Specialty is just what the name implies—a special show for our special breed. And the ingredient that makes it so special, such a very great honor to win, is that this show of shows affords Afghan Hound lovers and exhibitors the opportunity to support and promote the show especially dedicated to the glorification of the breed.

The first of the national Afghan Hound Specialty Shows was held in the month of June in 1940, with Dr. Eugene Beck awarding Best In Show honors in accordance with the standard for the breed used in England. It wasn't until September of 1948 that the Afghan Hound Club of America submitted and had accepted a clarification

Ch. Belden Bali Hi, owned, bred and shown by Leo Goodman. A son of Ch. Crown Crest Vegas Ghambler of Belden, Bali Hi is a proven stud and has an impressive show record to his credit. Photo by Lorenz.

Ch. Sahadi Scaramouche won a five-point major the first time shown at the Afghan Hound Club of America specialty Show in February 1962. He was best of winners, and best bred by exhibitor at this show. Sire: Ch. Shirkhan of Grandeur; dam: Ch. Crown Crest Khalifah. He was bred and is owned by the author. Photo by Evelyn Shafer.

of the English standard which became our American standard for the breed.

The Afghan Hound was a comparatively new and different breed to this country back in 1940 when the entrants at the first Specialty Show were seen by the public at the North Westchester Kennel Club show. And it was only through the concentrated efforts of such loyal and devoted supporters as Mrs. Sherman Hoyt, Mrs. Pamela Porter, Mrs. Jack Oakie, Mrs. Marion Foster Florsheim, Mrs. Leah McConaha, Mr. and Mrs. Robert Boger, Mr. and Mrs. Cyrus Rickel, Mr. and Mrs. Charles Wernsman, Dr. Eugene Beck, and Q. A. Shaw McKean that the breed began to flourish and grow to the point it has today.

Ch. Crown Crest Khalifah (fourth from left) pictured winning Brood Bitch class with five of her ten champion sons at the Afghan Hound Club of America Specialty Show in 1963. Khalifah was also Best of Opposite Sex to her son, Ch. Sahadi Shikari (fifth from left) as well as winner of the veteran Bitch class at this same Specialty. Pictured left to right are Ch. Sahadi Sessu, Ch. Sahadi Sinbad and Ch. Sahadi Scaramouche, Ch. Khalifah, Ch. Sahadi Shikari. At far right, is Ch. Sahadi Comanche Brave Eagle. This family portrait is a standing tribute to one of the top bitches of all time in the history of the breed. Photo by Evelyn Shafer.

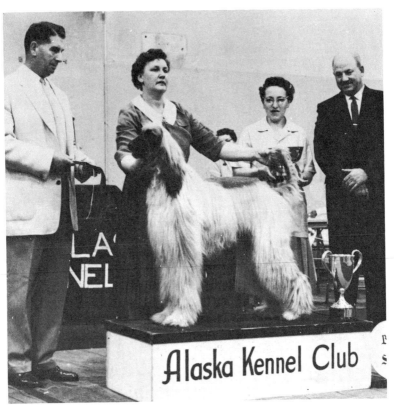

Ch. Hi Life Hi Bibbi, wins best in show at the Alaska Kennel Club. Judge Robert Waters presents the award to owner Margaret Webber.

Charlotte Coffey and, until her death in 1956, Mrs. Robert Boger, had served for many years as the club's secretaries. Miss Coffey, now 1st Vice President and incomparable Specialty Show chairman each year, is largely responsible for the success of this show annually. It is gratifying to note that each year entries increase substantially, attendance soars to new heights, the trophy lists add up like an inventory at a silversmith's shop, and the catalogue advertisements represent the social register of Afghandom.

By way of paying homage to some of our great show-winning Afghan Hounds, and by way of presenting a permanent record of Specialty winning dogs, we hereby acknowledge the Best In Show wins at our Specialty Shows since their inauguration in the year 1940:

If you decide to show your dog to any great extent you will find that
sooner or later you will have not only ribbons, but trophies for his
wins. The first one is usually proudly displayed on the mantlepiece in
the living room, but as they increase in numbers you will find you need
a bigger place for them. A trophy shelf in your kennel room can be
impressive, or trophies can be conversation pieces in your recreation
room, or as separators in your bookshelves.

AFGHAN HOUND CLUB OF AMERICA
SPECIALTY SHOW WINNERS

1940 CH. TANYAH SAHIB OF CY ANN
> Owners, Mr. and Mrs. Cyrus K. Rickel
> Judge, Dr. Eugene C. Beck
> N. Westchester, Katonah, New York
> June, 1940

1941 CH. HAZAR
> Owner, Dr. Gertrude Kinsey
> Judge, Dr. Arthur W. Combs
> N. Westchester, Katonah, New York
> June, 1941

Son of a famous son, of a famous son . . . Kaja's Silky Boy. This stylish son of Ch. Kora's King David, is also a grandson of Ch. Khabiri of Grandeur, and is owned by Karen and Julian Armistead. Photo by Evelyn Shafer.

1942 CH. RAJAH OF ARKEN
Owner, Charles A. Wernsman
Judge, Mrs. Robert F. Boger
N. Westchester, Katonah, New York
June, 1942

1943 CH. RAJAH OF ARKEN
Owner, Charles A. Wernsman
Judge, Dr. Gertrude Kinsey
N. Westchester, Rye, New York
June, 1943

1944 CH. RAJAH OF ARKEN
Owner, Charles A. Wernsman
Judge, Mrs. Jack Oakie
N. Westchester, Rye, New York
June, 1944

Ch. Mandith Alexander the Great, three year old winner of the Tara Afghan Hound Club Specialty Show in 1964 under judge Dr. William Waskow, handler, Michele Leathers. "Alex" also has five group placings to his credit. Owner Judith Fellton. Photo by Alexander.

American and Mexican Ch. Crown Crest Great Mogul, owned by Dr. A. L. Jenkines. He is shown taking best of breed at the San Antonio Kennel Club, handled by Maxine Beam, under the late Colonel E. E. Ferguson. Photo by Alexander.

1945 No Specialty Show (Government war restrictions on travel)

1946 CH. KARACH OF KHANHASSET
  Owner, Leah P. McConaha
  Judge, Robert F. Boger
  Interstate, Glen Cove, L.I., New York
  September, 1946

1947 CH. KARACH OF KHANHASSET
  Owner, Leah P. McConaha
  Judge, Charles A. Wernsman
  Hotel McAlpin, New York, New York
  February, 1947

1948 CH. KARAN OF KHANHASSET
Owner, Leah P. McConaha
Judge, Ernest E. Ferguson
Hotel McAlpin, New York, New York
February, 1948

CH. MAJARA MAHABAT
Owners, Mr. and Mrs. Frederick A. Jagger
Judge, Mrs. E. Ferguson McConaha
Interstate, Briarcliff, New York
September, 1948

1949 CH. MAJARA MAHABAT
Owners, Mrs. and Mrs. Frederick A. Jagger
Judge, Mrs. E. Ferguson McConaha
Hotel McAlpin, New York, New York
February, 1949

Ch. Crown Crest Khittiku, C.D., is owned by Patricia Sinden, Tajmir Kennels. This black-masked silver bitch finished for her championship with five major wins. Handled by Jack Funk, Khittiku has been an important breeding force at Mrs. Sinden's kennel. Photo by Frasie.

Ch. Sahadi Sinbad, owned by Sahadi Kennels, shown winning the hound group at the Rockland County Kennel Club show under judge Marjorie Siebern. This beautifully-coated dog is a son of Ch. Shirkhan of Grandeur and was bred by Joan Brearley. Photo by Evelyn Shafer.

Ch. Chinah of Grandeur, sire of the island of Puerto Rico's first Afghan Hound home-bred champion. Chinah, himself is a winner of 1 best in show and 5 hound group firsts in Puerto Rican competition. He is owned by Mr. and Mrs. Harley Miller.

Ch. Crown Crest Topaz, owned by Gordon and Conni Miller. He is one of the famous 'Gem' litter bred by Kay Finch. Toby was a top show winner in his own right, and has made his mark as a sire of champions. One son, Ch. High Life Hi Bibbi, owned by Margaret Webber, was a Best In Show winner in Alaska. Photo by Lockhart.

1950 CH. TURKUMAN NISSIM'S LAUREL
Owners, Sunny Shay and Sol Malkin
Judge, Alva Rosenberg
Hotel Belvedere, New York, New York
February, 1950

1951 CH. BLU ARABIS OF KUVERA
Owners, Lee and Howard Iverson
Judge, Cyrus K. Rickel
Hotel McAlpin, New York, New York
February, 1951

1952 KARLI BEN GHAZI
        Owners, Ruth H. Thom and J. E. Baird
        Judge, Alex Scott
        Hotel Henry Hudson, New York, New York
        February, 1952

1953 CH. MAJARA MIHRAB
        Owners, Mr. and Mrs. Frederick A. Jagger
        Judge, Dr. Arthur W. Combs
        Hotel Henry Hudson, New York, New York
        February, 1953

A headstudy of the beautiful Afghan Hound bitch, Thief's Mystery of Crown Crest, bred by Kay Finch.

Ch. Kora's King David, a spirited showman and sire, this flashy black dog was bred and is owned by Karen and Julian Armistead. Photo by Evelyn Shafer.

1954 CH. TAEJON OF CROWN CREST
  Owner, Kay Finch
  Judge, Chris Shuttleworth
  Hotel Henry Hudson, New York, New York
  February, 1954

1955 CH. KARLI BEN GHAZI
  Owners, Ruth H. Tongren and Josephine Baird
  Judge, Dr. Eugene C. Beck
  Hotel Henry Hudson, New York, New York
  February, 1955

1956 CH. LALA ROOKH OF ESTIOC
  Owner, Patricia D. Leary
  Judge, Mrs. Warner S. Hays
  Hotel Henry Hudson, New York, New York
  February, 1956

Ch. Tarawazir of Carloway Crown Crest pictured with co-owner Kay Finch and judge Hollis Wilson at the Beverly Riviera Kennel Club Show. Wazir was bred at Sheila Devitt's Carloway Kennels in England. He is now co-owned and campaigned by Alma L. Wells and Mrs. Finch.

Ch. Sahadi Saan, one of the champions at Sahadi Kennels. He is another son of the famous Ch. Taejon of Crown Crest out of Ch. Crown Crest Khalifah.

1957 CH. CROWN CREST ZARDONX
Owner, Kay S. Finch
Judge, Mrs. Lauer J. Froelich
Hotel Henry Hudson, New York, New York
February, 1957

1958 CH. CROWN CREST ZARDONX
Owner, Kay S. Finch
Judge, Miss Anna Katherine Nicholas
Hotel Henry Hudson, New York, New York
February, 1958

1959 CH. SHIRKHAN OF GRANDEUR
Owners, Sunny Shay and Dorothy Chenade
Judge, Mr. Cyrus K. Rickel
Hotel Henry Hudson, New York, New York
February, 1959

1960 CH. CROWN CREST MR. UNIVERSE
Owners, Kay S. Finch and Chas. A. Costabile
Judge, Mr. Robert F. Boger
Hotel Henry Hudson, New York, New York
February, 1960

1961 CH. HOLLY HILL DRACO
Owner, Sue A. Kauffman
Judge, Mr. Percy Roberts
Hotel Henry Hudson, New York, New York
February, 1961

1962 CH. AKABA'S TOP BRASS
Owner, Lois R. Boardman
Judge: Dr. Wm. L. Waskow
Hotel Henry Hudson, New York, New York
February, 1962

1963 CH. SAHADI SHIKARI
Owner, Dr. and Mrs. E. F. Winter
Judge, Mrs. Braden Finch
Hotel Henry Hudson, New York, New York
February, 1963

1964 CH. TAJMIR'S REDSTONE ROCKET
Owner, Patricia Sinden
Judge, Mrs. Sherman Hoyt
Hotel Henry Hudson, New York, New York

Ch. Kareb Larookh, owned and handled by Alma L. Wells, is shown winning the hound group at the Hunterdon Hills Kennel Club under judge Lewis Worden. Photo by Evelyn Shafer.

American and Canadian Ch. Crown Crest Mr. California, owned by Forrest Hansen and Donald McIlvain. At three years of age, Mr. California has 5 all-breed best in show wins and 28 hound group firsts on his show record. He was top hound in Canada for 1963. Sired by American and Canadian Champion Crown Crest Mr. Universe, the top winning Afghan Hound of all time, his dam is Ch. Crown Crest Eve Queen.

194

Membership in the Afghan Hound Club of America, Inc. is by sponsorship of two current members in good standing and election by the Board of Directors. As in most clubs, there are annual dues and the annual meetings for general club activities, followed by one of four annual meetings of the club officers and Board of Directors. This annual meeting follows the judging of the Specialty Show at Henry Hudson Hotel in New York City each February.

In addition to the annual meeting following the Specialty Show on the Sunday preceding the Westminster Kennel Club event, the club holds an outdoor Match Show each Fall with A.K.C. sanction. The first of these Match Shows was held on September 26th, 1941, at Marion Foster Florsheim's Five Mile Kennels in Connecticut, with John H. Hill judging. Mrs. Sherman Hoyt's Rudika of Blakeen was Best In Match, also winning the honor of being first Afghan Hound Club of America Match Show winner.

Int. Ch. Tanjores Domino winning at an American dog show under judge Maurice Baker. Domino had already won championship titles in Norway, Sweden, Finland and Austria. The owner, Mrs. John Guzevich, is handling. Photo by Joan Ludwig.

Ch. Mazur I Sherief of Moornistan, owned by Harold O'Rynn. This lovely black and silver group winner is son of the Westminster Kennel Club best in show winner, Ch. Shirkhan of Grandeur.

The parent club became incorporated on November 17, 1950. After this date it was known as the Afghan Hound Club of America; it was originally called simply the Afghan Hound Club. For the first several years the Specialty Shows were held in conjunction with the North Westchester Kennel Club shows. February 1947 was the first of the independent Specialties and was held at the Hotel McAlpin in New York City.

Club secretaries change from year to year, so those desiring name and address of the current club officers should get in touch with the American Kennel Club for the address of the current officer serving as Secretary.

REGIONAL CLUBS

When the Afghan Hound in all its elegance and beauty began to take a strong foothold in this country, the formation of regional clubs to serve members who could not make the annual pilgrimage to the New York headquarters became inevitable.

Ch. Babur-Ben of Kubera, winner of 5 Hound Groups and 20 group placings to date. Owner-handler-breeder Harold O'Rynn. Photo by William Brown.

One of the largest and most active of all regional clubs is the Afghan Hound Club of California, which held its first annual Specialty Show in 1948. There is also a Northern California Afghan Hound Club; this club held its first annual Specialty Show in conjunction with the Golden Gate Kennel Club at the Civic Auditorium in San Francisco in January of 1958.

In the Mid-West there is, appropriately enough, the Mid-West Afghan Hound Club; this organization, which held its first Specialty Show in 1958, holds its annual Specialty the day of the Ravenna (Ohio) Kennel Club show. In 1959 the Afghan Hound Club of Greater Chicago was formed with a large and active membership.

A pensive Ch. Shahti Ben Kajar, pictured at nine months of age. Owner Mary Sheldon.

Ch. Harleana's Mukhalla El Wahid, owned by Harley Miller, Jr. He is shown here winning best of breed under judge Mrs. A. Van Court at Ravenna and on to Group 3rd. Ben Burwell is the handler. Wahid is the first home-bred Afghan Hound champion from Puerto Rico. Photo by Norton of Kent.

The Potomac Afghan Hound Club usually stages its Specialty Show of late along with the National Capital Kennel Club show in Washington, D.C. Originally it was called the Eastern Afghan Hound Club. This club was formed on August 15, 1948, at the home of Mr. and Mrs. Ward M. French, with sixteen members present. Mrs. Howard Jackson was elected first president. In 1949 the club sponsored the Afghan Hound entry at the National Capital show, as it does to this day, but their first Specialty Show was in 1950, held in conjunction with the Old Dominion Kennel Club show.

There is also the Tara Afghan Hound Club, with headquarters in Atlanta, Georgia; this club held its first annual Specialty in 1956. In the early 1960's we saw the appearance of the Afghan Hound Club of Detroit, the Florida Club, and most recent of all, the Colonial

Ch. Sahadi Comanche Brave Eagle, a black-masked apricot dog owned by Chet and Ellen O'Leske. Photo by Stephen Klein.

International Champion Tanjores Domino pictured with Sandy Moore, Miss New Mexico for 1964. This shot was used as publicity for the Atlantic City Miss America pageant. Owned by Mr. and Mrs. J. J. Guzevich, Domino has won championships all over Europe and in the U.S.A. as well.

Afghan Hound Club in the New England area.

Many members of these regional clubs are also members of the parent club, thereby assuring a very close association with all breeders, owners, and exhibitors of all parts of the nation. It is a wonderful way of keeping up with Afghan Hound activities, and all the members are devoted to the concept that through mutual friendship and cooperation the popularity and good of all Afghan Hounds will be preserved.

AFGHAN HOUND PUBLICATIONS

An important way of maintaining the closeness and cooperation of these clubs is through the various informative bulletins and publications composed and distributed by the various clubs and organizations to their memberships.

Though the earliest records of the history of the Afghan Hound were written on papyrus, down through the centuries scattered and varied accounts of the breed and its illustrious history have been passed along by other means as well. Today, for instance, there are many recommended sources for the fancier desiring to learn more about the breed.

Ch. Zaamarakuri of Ghazni, owned by Mary Kenney.

Ch. Swedika Joh-Cyn, bred and owned by Mrs. Cynthia Guzevich, is a beautiful example of an exquisite black and tan Afghan Hound. She is shown winning best of opposite sex for two points enroute to her championship. The judge was Richard L. Fried and the handler was the late Roland Muller. Photo by Joan Ludwig.

The author with her Ch. Crown Crest Jesi Jhaimz preparing to enter the ring at the famous Morris and Essex Kennel Club. This great show is no longer in existence, but when it was operating, Afghan Hounds often accounted for major wins at this canine extravaganza.

Almost all of the leading dog magazines carry a breed column each month wherein a member of the club writes and informs readers of breed activities. Most of these magazines can be purchased at the larger newstands or by subscription from the magazine itself:

American Kennel Gazette, 51 Madison Avenue, New York, New York.

Popular Dogs Magazine, 2009 Ranstead Street, Philadelphia 3, Pennsylvania.

Dog World, 469 East Ohio Street, Chicago 11, Illinois.

Kennel Review, 229 S. Glendale Avenue, Glendale, California.

I would also like to call special attention to two extra special issues of *Popular Dogs Magazine*, which turned over two complete issues of this excellent publication to the Afghan Hound. Copies of the June, 1950 and June, 1956 issues were devoted to the Afghan Hound in particular. I believe these two issues are sold out, but many members of the clubs have extra copies that can be borrowed to acquaint

Group and Specialty winner, Ch. Gandhi of Lakoya owned by Mrs. John Jeffrey. This exotic pure white Afghan Hound carries an amber saddle and the desired dark pigmentation, with silky flowing coat. Photo by Roberts.

Ch. Samaris of Moornistan shown here with handler Tom Crowe. "Sammi" had a remarkable show career, with five group firsts and many group placings on her record. Retired to motherhood in 1960, Sammi has produced many champion offspring, including best in show and group winners.

Ch. Sahadi Sabrina, black-masked silver daughter of Ch. Taejon of Crown Crest and Ch. Crown Crest Khalifah. Sabrina is a foundation bitch at the author's Sahadi Kennels.

Afghan Hound lovers with much of the lore about our breed both past and present. As columnist for *Popular Dogs* for over five years now, I heartily recommend that you be sure to obtain copies of the June issue of this magazine each year. It is a special Hound issue and always provides a wealth of pictures and material on our breed.

Another magazine that Afghan Hound fanciers and breeders will be benefited by is *All-Pets*, published monthly by T.F.H. Publications.

Although the Afghan Hound was originally a hunter, he gets along well with other animals in the home. Here two eastern beauties relax in each other's company.

El Citono Del Desierto, or "Tono," is another of Pearson Crosby's hunting Afghan Hounds, from his Del Desierto Kennels.

Marion Foster Florsheim and Int. Ch. Rudika of Blakeen visit the editor of the Saturday Evening Post magazine to discuss the magazine cover displayed in the background, featuring three of Mrs. Florsheim's famous Afghan Hounds. This March 18th, 1944 cover marked the first color cover on the Post, and the first time a dog was on the cover. Rutherford Boyd was the artist.

SHOW RING TERMINOLOGY

If you show your dog, win or lose, you will enjoy reading about the show results in the various newspapers and magazines. In these reports, you will find many abbreviated show ring terms used that you should be familiar with if you are to correctly interpret the results. A list of the most frequently used terms are as follows:

BIS	best in show
BOS	best of opposite sex
GR1, GR2, etc.	first, second, third or fourth place in each group
BOB	best of breed
WD or WB	winners dog or winners bitch
RD or RB	reserve winners dog or bitch
Am-bred	bred in America

BBE	bred by exhibitor
BIM	best in match
Ch.	champion of record

When there are color classifications in the various breeds, abbreviated terms also are used.

R/W	red and white
Bl/T	black and tan
Bl/W	black and white

If you intend to enter your dog in obedience or in field trials, you will find equally as many abbreviations used.

There can be no doubt that the great beauty and exotic aspect of the Afghan Hound have projected him as a major breed in the show ring. Today he is one of the most important breeds in the hound group. Photo by Three Lions.

OTC	obedience trial club
CD	companion dog degree
CDX	companion dog excellent
UD	utility dog degree
TD	tracking dog
UDT	utility dog tracker
01, 02, etc.	placings in open class
N1, N2, etc.	placings in novice class
GN1, GN2, etc.	graduate novice placings
TT	tracking test

The two most frequently seen in field reports are:

F.T.Ch.	field trial champion
Dual Ch.	bench and field champion

Ch. Tajmir Bhi-Jhupiter, is a black-masked apricot son of Ch. Karli ben-ghaZi out of Ch. Crown Crest Khittiku, C.D. "Jupiter" is shown here before finishing his championship, winning the local Hound Group at the Stone City Kennel Club, at sixteen months of age with handler Bill Irwin. Jupiter was bred and is owned by Patricia Sinden, Tajmir Kennels. Photo by Carl Glanz.

A typical and delightful pose of an Afghan Hound puppy. Zaamadhar of Stormhill, owned and bred by Gini Withington. Photo by Joan Ludwig.

If a dog is imported from another country, you will often find that the letters Imp. precede or follow his name. When a dog has been campaigned, or has attained a championship title in other countries, his name is preceded by abbreviations of the names of the countries in which such championship status has been earned—as in the illustrious series of titles which name Kay Finch's famous imported stud dog, Amer., Belg., Dutch, Germ., Ch. Ophaal of Crown Crest. While Ophaal is referred to as an International Champion, the names of the countries must be listed in his "legal" name. The abbreviations used for two other countries are Can. for Canada, and Mex. for Mexico.

THE AFGHAN HOUND COMMANDMENTS

1. Thou shalt remember that thou art an Afghan Hound, let no man change thee.
2. Thou shalt not walk like a duck, but with thy feet out straight.
3. Thou shalt not look like an owl, with large light eyes.
4. Thou shalt carry thy saddle with pride, for it is a true badge of thy breed.
5. Thou shalt carry thy tail high, and with ring.
6. Thou shalt not have a nose like unto a hawk.
7. Thou shalt move without thy hocks knocking.
8. Thou shalt carry thyself with power and grace, for thou art the hound of antiquity.
9. Thou shalt not believe that only thy color is proper, for all colors are equal.
10. Thou shalt not cover thy faults with excess coat, for thy faults shall be handed down to thy children and to their children.

ANONYMOUS

BIBLIOGRAPHY

American Kennel Club. "Complete Dog Book". New York: Garden City Press, 1956.

Ash, Edward C. "Dogs: Their History and Development".

Baillie-Grohman. "15th Century Sporting Dogs", *Connoisseur*, Vol. 9. London: 1904.

Breasted, James A. "Ancient Records of Egypt". Vol. 4. Chicago: 1906-1907.

Ceram, C. W. "Gods, Graves and Scholars". New York: Alfred A. Knopf, 1952.

Champollion. "A History of Famous Dogs".

Colbert, Edwin H. "Natural History". Vol. 43. New York, 1939.

Davis, Henry P., Editor. "The Modern Dog Encyclopedia". Harrisburg, Pa.: The Stackpole Co., 1956.

Fielding, William J. "Strange Superstitions and Magical Practices". Philadelphia: Circle Books, 1945.

Griffith, Beatrice Fox. "Dog History". 1890.

Herrmann, Paul. Conquest by Man. New York: Harper and Brothers, 1954.

Hubbard, Clifford. "The Afghan Hound". London: Nicolson and Watson, 1951.

Mason, Walter Esplin. "Dogs of All Nations".

Popular Dogs Magazine. June, 1950, June, 1956.

Sanford, Jackson K. "Science Finds Afghan Still Has Primitive Body Structure". Cited in *Popular Dogs*, June 1956, p. 30.

Srinivasan, V. "Canine Friends of the Great". *New Review*, 1942.

Wilson, Gilbert Livingston. "The Horse and the Dog in Hidatsa Culture". 1924.

INDEX

(Dog names are given without titles)